Home in the Church

HOME
in the
CHURCH

Living an Embodied Catholic Faith

JESSICA PTOMEY

NEW YORK

LONDON • NASHVILLE • MELBOURNE • VANCOUVER

Home in the Church
Living an Embodied Catholic Faith

Published in New York, New York, by Morgan James Publishing. Morgan James is a trademark of Morgan James, LLC. www.MorganJamesPublishing.com

ISBN 9781642797084 paperback
ISBN 9781642797091 eBook
Library of Congress Control Number: 2019944907

Cover Design by:
Megan Dillon
megan@creativeninjadesigns.com

Interior Design by:
Christopher Kirk
www.GFSstudio.com

To my husband,
Mike.
Thank you for helping me find home and living
this journey with me.

To my children,
Tyler, Walker, Samuel, and Stella Maris.
May you always be home in the Catholic Church.

Contents

Preface

There is a common sentiment among converts that becoming Catholic is like *coming home*. I had known and loved Christ my whole life, but not until age thirty did I discover and come to love His "holy Catholic and apostolic Church." And it is my active life within His Church that has drawn me closer to the reality of my eternal home with Him. Ultimately, my faith's home is in the Catholic Church because she shows me how *not* to be at home on this earth. She points me continually to heaven through her liturgies, sacraments, prayers, teachings, and traditions. Though a shelter of great protection and solace, she disrupts my tendencies to be contented with the ends of this world. She is the tangible and tactile vessel that is carrying me faithfully to my *eternal* destination…leading me ever homeward.

From the Hall to Home

I grew up with Awanas and Missionnettes, Vacation Bible Schools and summer youth camps, Sunday School and Wednesday night Youth Group. I attended Bryan College, founded by William Jennings Bryan of the famous Scopes Monkey Trials, in Dayton, TN. I did my graduate work at Pat Robertson's Regent University, where I met my husband, Mike. By all accounts, I am a product of Evangelicalism; and I have it to thank for many good and great experiences in my life—the greatest of which is my personal relationship with Jesus Christ.

I would describe my former self as an "Evangelical" because that umbrella was a constant in my Christian upbringing, much more so than the ever-changing denomination of the church we were currently attending. Throughout my childhood and adolescence my family attended numerous and divergent Protestant churches. My experience moving in and out of various Christian denominations and experiencing the theological differences and disunity of them all was perhaps the greatest impetus for my openness to Catholicism. In my late twenties, as my husband and I specifically questioned aspects of Protestantism, I consciously went through a period I can only describe as "nomadic faith." I felt *homeless*. During this period of searching, all I had to hold on to was Christ and what C. S. Lewis describes as *"Mere" Christianity*—basic Orthodox faith. I never lost that, though many post-Evangelicals my age had left Orthodoxy behind completely. That mere Christian faith offered a *shelter* during our faith journey, but not a *home*. I now realize that I had actually been living under this "lean-to" much of my Christian life. I am desperately grateful for it, as many people have no gift of inherited faith at all; but as Lewis observes, affirmation of those basic tenets of Christian Orthodoxy is not meant to be a substitute for participating in a particular creed and communion. "It is more like a hall out of which doors open into several rooms...," says Lewis, "but it is in the rooms, not in the hall, that there are fires and chairs and meals. The hall is a place to wait in, a place from which to try the various doors, not a place to live in."[1]

I didn't realize before that I had been living in the "hall" most of my life. I needed a *home* for my faith, not just a shelter or a lean-to to get me by. I knew instinctively that the concept of "church" was important, that we were not meant to be spiritually "homeless" people. I was not sure what the Church was supposed to look like. I was pretty sure the structures I had experienced growing up were missing important elements, but that did not mean the Church established by Jesus Christ in the first century no longer existed; the fact that my soul was seeking it made me think it *must* exist. And if it did exist, I would know it when I found it, because I would encounter the fullness of Christ there.

Searching for the truth often involves a period of waiting; and looking for a home means you will be wandering for some amount of time. My husband and I waited, homelessly, for about six years in the hall of our mere Christian faith. As we entered different doors one by one, we found ourselves being led through various passageways that kept connecting back to the same room—the Catholic Church. We entered to a vibrant fire that had been burning since Christ's apostles walked the earth, to ancient chairs that had held saints from centuries before, and to a Eucharistic meal that fed souls like no other. We knew we had found a place in which to live, a home for our faith, because we encountered Christ in that room more fully than we ever had before. We had no need to go back into the hall; our waiting was over. We had found Mother Church, and we were ready to start living in this new home.

Introduction

My desire is to take you on a journey with me of discovering Catholicism as the *home* it is meant to be—the sacramental, liturgical, life-giving dwelling where we encounter Christ. But to do that, we have to understand what kind of home it is; and we have to realize that it is a fundamentally different place to live and *way* of living than we may be accustomed to in modern American culture. The Holy Spirit drew me into the Church through many avenues of grace—the ancient liturgy, the sacramental theology, and the various rituals and traditions. However, coming out of the hall and into my new home in the Catholic Church did not mean I automatically knew how to live in it. There is a difference between acquiring intellectual knowledge that leads you through the doors of Catholicism and becoming an active participant in the revealed truth—*living in it*. Catholic practices and rituals were not suddenly intuitive the day I was confirmed. With practice, they would become more and more automatic in my faith life over time; but other intuitions would also have to become *unpracticed* over time.

Growing up in modern American culture, most of us have inherited a Christian faith that is interwoven with modernist thought; so we tend to view elements of our world, our faith included, according to principles that stem from the Enlightenment—namely, that all truth is reduced to observable, non-paradoxical collections of facts that impact our lives by our thinking about them. (Remember Descartes' mantra, "I think; therefore, I am"?) Because a modernist approach is so ingrained in our culture, we automatically approach daily Christian life from this assumption that we are primarily thinking beings—disembodied brains on stick figures—and we are actually no more aware of this operating assumption than we are aware of the very air we breathe moment by moment. It's the norm.

Philosophy of religion scholar James K. A. (Jamie) Smith aptly summarizes the impact modernism has had on the life of our faith: "Modern Christianity tends to think of the church either as a place where individuals come to find answers to their questions or as one more stop where individuals can try to satisfy their consumerist desires."[2] Strains of American Protestantism have particularly deep roots in modernistic thinking;[3] and though the Catholic Church's foundation in ancient Christian thought and practice provides a stark contrast to modernistic expressions of American Christianity, many modern Catholics and Catholic institutions have been significantly impacted by a modernist mindset as well.

Our journey toward a "lived-in" Catholic faith cannot be primarily approached as a job for the intellect, in hopes that *understanding* the theological arguments and truth of the sacraments and liturgy will automatically transmit their impact in our lives. It is actually the *practice* of our Catholicism that will transform our Catholic identities. There is a poignant saying attributed to Saint Francis de Sales: "You learn to speak by speaking, to study by studying, to run by running, to work by working, and just so, you learn to love by loving. All those who think to learn in any other way deceive themselves." What St. Francis is describing is an *embodied faith*—a faith that is realized in the practice of it.

Let me give you a practical example of how powerful this concept of embodiment is. During one epic Maryland winter storm (we are talking four feet of snow), I had my garage all moved around to accommodate our van and truck, plus everything else that was already in the garage. It was a tight fit, and we had to arrange everything in sort of a puzzle to get it all in there. I had to walk around the truck, squeezing by, to put things in the trash or recycle bins for about two weeks. It was a pain, and I couldn't wait to get the truck moved out and the garage back to normal once all the snow had been removed. However, the day I moved everything back, I started walking the wrong direction to put bags in the trash—I had learned a new habit (whether I liked it or not), and *intellectually knowing* that the trash cans were back in their original locations did not automatically translate to me *walking* to that location. If this is what can happen with my practice of taking out the trash, what are the implications for the practice of spiritual habits and our worship of God?

My understanding of *embodied faith* took shape in 2009, toward the middle of six years of church "homelessness," and this discovery was actually a strong catalyst for me beginning to consider the Catholic Church. I was completing my doctoral dissertation when, through my research, I realized how much my Christian faith, in practice and belief, had been impacted by modernist presuppositions (those assumptions about the world that we bring to all of our experiences). I engaged the question: *If modernism has set much of Christianity on the wrong path, then how do we get back to a more faithful one?* I found the answer in reading Jamie Smith's work on cultural liturgies. He says that since we are not first and foremost "thinking beings," but rather, "desiring beings," we were created to *love*. We were created to think as well, obviously; but we were created *in love* and *for love* in the first place. Smith goes on to say that what we love we *worship*, and we all worship *something*.[4] And what is it that determines our love? Our *habits*. What we repeatedly do, what we practice over and over again, is the thing that makes evident and real our love and our worship. An embodied faith is rooted in the concept that "we feel our way around our world more than we think our way through it."[5]

My paradigm was being turned on its head. *So, it's less about how much I think about and study Christian doctrine that makes me a Christian, and more about how I habitually practice it?* This predisposition for humans to worship *something* suddenly became clear; for, as Smith points out with the examples of the *shopping mall* and *the sports arena,* "religious" people are not the only ones who worship, because they aren't the only ones who love.[6] All human beings were created to desire and to worship, and in our modern culture it is so normal and natural to worship material possessions and athletic gods. Smith, a Protestant scholar, is citing and developing concepts of the human person that originated back with one of our Doctors of the Church, St. Thomas Aquinas. Aquinas said that what a person's *will* takes pleasure in is what determines whether or not that person is virtuous: "… that man is good and virtuous, who takes pleasure in the works of virtue; and that man evil, who takes pleasure in evil works."[7] Dr. Peter Kreeft paraphrases Aquinas beautifully: *"The things that we love tell us what we are."*[8]

If we *love* material possessions, then we will know it by how much stuff we buy; and if we *love* sports or various other entertainments, then we will know it by how much time we give to them. The connections to material possessions and how we spend our free time were pretty clear to me, but my previous experience of "church" seemed disconnected from this embodied concept of worship. *Did such an embodied expression of faith (missing from my own modern church experiences) actually exist, and had it existed for centuries?* I found that indeed it had as I investigated the liturgy, sacramental theology, and traditions of the Catholic Church. From the beginning of Christianity, centuries before modernity, the Catholic Church has preserved this understanding that our "worship" of God is connected to us habitually practicing our love for Him in various embodied ways. But if we have bought into a modernist view of our faith without realizing it, then we will not naturally recognize the embodied nature of our Catholic faith, and we certainly will not live in it to our full potential.

Living an Embodied Catholic Faith

In the following chapters, I share several primary environments in which I have experienced Catholicism's rich embodied faith: the liturgy of the Mass, the sacraments of the church, the life of the Catholic family, the liturgical year, the life of prayer, and the times of suffering. The *living out* of Catholic teachings and traditions in these environments has drawn me closer to Christ and fixed my heart on my eternal destiny; and I believe it can do the same for you. An embodied Catholic faith will change us—change us from being *individual consumers* to *collective participants* in the life and home of the Church. As we go, remember that this kind of change means engaging our will, as St. Thomas Aquinas said. Our intellect will direct us where to go, but our will has to get us there. We are seeking communion with God, both now and throughout eternity. We want to faithfully worship—with our whole beings—the God who created us for love, because He desired a relationship with us and wants us to desire the same with Him. We are practicing here on earth what we will spend all eternity experiencing in perfection. I offer the following prayer for us on this journey:

> *May living an embodied Catholic faith draw us into the depths of the Father's love for us; may we share in Christ's life as we share in the life of His Church; and may the Holy Spirit always guide Mother Church, our home on earth, to move us toward our heavenly home, the one for which we have been created. Amen.*

chapter 1

The Mass: Embodied Faith in Worship

"When we begin to see that heaven awaits us in the Mass, we begin already to bring our home to heaven. And we begin already to bring heaven home with us." —Scott Hahn[9]

Discovering the Mass

Protestant Sunday morning worship experiences can look vastly different across America, depending on the church's denomination. As I have mentioned, my family had been members or attendees of numerous churches and denominations while I was growing up. One of the reasons for frequently changing churches was that we moved a lot—I count eleven times since I was born until I went to grad school. (No, we weren't a military family.) The other, and more significant, reason was that my parents were earnestly seeking *correct* Christian doctrines and the expression of those doctrines in the life and worship of the local church. You see, while my parents grew up in nominally Christian homes as children (the Presbyterian/Baptist and Episcopal traditions), their early adult lives were void of any personal faith. They both had dramatic conversions to Christ around their thirties, and they spent the years following sincerely searching for some solid foundations when it came to doctrine and Christian life. Unfortunately, human moral failure appears in every Christian tradition. Between experiencing a few pastoral scandals here and there, as well as bumping into problematic theological teachings or doctrine that went off the rails from orthodoxy completely, our family ended up all over the spectrum. I've experienced just about every type of denomination and worship service expression throughout my childhood, from fundamentalist Baptist churches to lively charismatic fellowships. You name it, I've seen it. The only expression of worship that I had *not* experienced was a liturgical service.

My husband's experience was much more consistent. He grew up in the Assembly of God denomination, at the same church his whole life. When we married in 2005, we decided that we would start our life together back in Mike's hometown, and we ended up making his childhood church our church home for the next two years. We experienced a wonderful community of Christians who cared deeply for us, since most of them had known Mike his whole life. And they all accepted me with much warmth and love. This was quite a foreign experience for me when it came to a church community, simply because the longest we had been at one church was during my high school years. Even then, there was more of a connection for me and my siblings with our youth group than there was for our whole family in the life of that large Southern Baptist church.

Mike and I ended up leaving his childhood church in 2007. Though there were a variety of reasons for our choice, we had ultimately been wrestling for months with a few important questions: *What is Sunday morning supposed to be? What is the local church supposed to look like? What is worship?* Now we were both raised in church, had been educated at Christian schools, had numerous Bible studies under our belts, and had been involved heavily in youth group and college ministries. We had even considered being part of a couple of different church plants. It's not like we were newbies asking these questions. Quite the opposite. We were young adults raised in the Evangelical tradition who greatly cherished our faith in Christ, but we were realizing that there were some major gaps between the Church and her worship of God that we read about in Scripture and the structure of most Sunday morning services that we had experienced. At this point, we hadn't yet discovered that our core struggles were actually Protestant/Catholic issues. Our questions seemed to be more in regard to stylistic observances about the format of many Evangelical worship services. (Though we soon discovered that questions of substance were really at the heart of various issues that appeared, on the surface, to be about style.)

Sometimes it's difficult to analyze a faith tradition while participating in it, and we realized (soberly) that we needed a break from church. I don't remember exactly how long we stopped attending Sunday services; maybe it was a few months. We finally ended up at a popular and large "community church," just to have somewhere to worship on Sundays and have space to consider what was next. We had friends who were asking similar questions, and we often discussed shared concerns and convictions until late in the evening. We had considered the model of "house churches" and various other church plants that were popping up here and there. There seemed to be post-Evangelical authors writing all the time about new models for "doing church"—some ideas sounded plausible; some sent us running in the opposite direction. I was nearing the end of my PhD program, and Mike (continually considering a pastoral call) was contemplating a PhD in theology from Fuller Theological Seminary in Los Angeles, a place he had long wanted to attend. We had talked about California many times, and we finally just made the leap. Mike was granted a "sabbatical" year from his teaching position at DeMatha Catholic High School (his alma mater), and off we went across the country to see what new vision the West Coast had to offer us. We would give it a year, and Mike would know after a few classes at Fuller if this was really what he wanted to do. As it turns out, we knew after about six months that this program wasn't it, and we planned to finish out the year there (while I defended my dissertation and graduated) and then head back to Maryland and start a family. But our time in California had offered us exactly the space the Holy Spirit wanted to expand our concept of "worship."

We experienced our first liturgical service at an Episcopal church in Pasadena, CA. The liturgy was a completely new experience for me. Standing in the beautiful church, I felt a new *awareness* of my role in worship. I whispered to Mike at various points that it didn't feel like we were members of a passive "audience" the way it felt at a lot of other churches, especially ones that seemed geared toward entertaining the people in the seats. The space was distinctly sacred and reverent; you would not confuse what was happening there with any other type of event. The congregation verbally responded throughout the liturgy, stood for the Gospel reading, and knelt in a receptive posture near the altar to partake of communion from the priest's hands. Everyone was *participating* in the liturgy; and I noticed that all the intentional elements of ritual pointed to Christ—both Christ in Scripture and Christ in Communion.

We visited this Episcopal church a handful of times that year, and each time I would try to decipher why the liturgical rituals of the service—and my participation in them—were so significant. It was during this time that I was studying Smith's work on cultural liturgies for my dissertation, particularly the concept that we are first and foremost *desiring* beings, not primarily thinking beings. I was realizing that it is our hearts, not our heads, that are fundamental in our spiritual formation, in our development of the "religious sense." Smith was telling me that I don't love things because I've thought a lot about them; I love what I worship.[10] *But what is worship?* This was the primary question I had been asking, and Smith helped me discover what I had been bumping up against but was unable to articulate—worship is embodied and liturgical. It is ritual. It is that thing that is practiced until it becomes habit. Our worship of God does not automatically stem from filling our minds with facts about God, but rather it is the agency of our prayers and bodies in the liturgy that actually put us in the posture of worship. The physical and vocal rituals that I was participating in on those Sunday mornings were actually forming my faith, forming my desire for God.

Despite the fact that we were starting to make these connections between worship and liturgy, we church hopped quite a bit during our time in LA. We hadn't quite given up on the Evangelical (or post-Evangelical) church plant model, and we decided to attend one that friends of ours had started once we moved back to Maryland in the summer of 2010. In hindsight, it was our "last hoorah" with Evangelical church culture (lasting a couple of years); the same problems kept repeating themselves. It wasn't long until we started feeling a pull back to the liturgy that we had experienced in California, only by this time we had actually followed the history of the liturgy back to its genesis—the Catholic Church and the Mass.

It's not that we didn't have a general knowledge of Church history all along. We obviously knew things were different before the Reformation (although my upbringing basically deprived me of fifteen hundred years of Church history). It was just that *becoming Catholic* was not on our radar...until we started actually befriending practicing Catholics and reading persuasive conversion stories,[11] and we realized that we couldn't avoid looking into the Catholic answer to all of these questions of worship and doctrine. We thought we should do our due diligence and leave no stone unturned. However, upon our cursory investigation, all of these liturgical traditions seemed to have the important elements of worship in common. In our estimate, Anglicans, Episcopalians, and Catholics were similar enough for us to avoid swimming the Tiber in order to practice a more liturgical and embodied faith. *Maybe we can just become Anglican*, we mused to ourselves.

About the same time, we became friends with the pastor (and his wife) of a small local Anglican church plant. It was a group of lovely people, formerly Evangelicals like us, who had been drawn to the beauty and embodied worship of the liturgy as well. It was a blessing to be part of that community while we continued to learn about the liturgy. But our reading, relationships with Catholic friends, and contemplation of the Eucharist had us considering the Catholic Mass more and more. My husband began having mystical encounters with the tabernacle in the school chapel at DeMatha. He didn't realize at the time that the consecrated Host was kept inside, and he wondered why he would feel "a warmth" the closer he sat to it. Needless to say, when he found out what it was he considered Catholicism in earnest. The Eucharist was always a primary question in the back of our minds, and we gradually grew more certain of our ultimate conclusion: *If that is the real body and blood of Christ, then we have to become Catholic!*

It was the spring of 2013, and I was *very* pregnant with our second child, due at the end of April. Mike and I had been seriously investigating Catholicism for several months. I had just finished reading Scott and Kimberly Hahn's conversion story, *Rome Sweet Home*.

We had binge-watched Robert Barron's *Catholicism* series, making the move to the Catholic Church more and more plausible with every episode. Most importantly, we realized that the sacrifice of the Mass—the Eucharist—was the center of the liturgy and of worship. All signs, both in Scripture and Church tradition, pointed to that focal point.

"I'm becoming Catholic," Mike announced to me one day. "And I hope you are ready too."

We had been married long enough that I knew what that meant. When my husband decided to do something, it would be happening in the *immediate* future.

"Okay, okay," I said. "I'm with you. Let's just have this baby and then figure out what the next step is."

"Nope. I don't want to wait."

He was firm. He knew, and he didn't want to waste any more time. Not every couple that enters the Catholic Church does so on the same timeline, and I am so thankful that we were on the same page all along. I have gone back in my mind to that moment so many times since we became Catholic, and my heart overflows with gratitude for the grace to trust in my husband's certainty. I tend to be the measured one; he likes to run headlong into what he *knows* is the right direction. I'd like to wait for the boat to come close enough to step in gently; he'd much rather jump. I'm so glad he was ready to jump; and I'm glad that I jumped with him. Because I listened to my husband, three months later we stood surrounded by glorious mural-covered walls at Holy Comforter-St. Cyprian Roman Catholic Church in Washington, DC, being confirmed side by side, witnessing both our boys being baptized, and receiving the Eucharist *together* for the first time.

Embodied Faith in the Mass

If I could condense into one statement all of my convictions about the structural and stylistic problems with most of the worship services of my pre-Catholic faith, it would be this: worship is *not* about us. It seems strange to have to clarify this point, to have to remind ourselves that we, the body of Christ, are gathering to worship *God*. Yet the clarification is needed, since the structure and design of many current Sunday services seem crafted to appeal to the sensibilities of those attending, to offer some sort of therapeutic message that lifts people's spirits and helps them live a better life. But such ends are not the *purpose* of worship, though they should indeed be a by-product of it. Many Christian services have become—in style and substance—an accessory to a highly commercialized life of faith. Mind you, this has not just happened in Evangelical and mainline Protestant churches. Many Catholic parishes are trending in this direction as well, rejecting the liturgical guidelines from church traditions and documents that have guided the liturgy of the Mass since its beginning (as early as the first century). If we do not understand exactly what the liturgy is, and its role in the practice of our faith, then we may become susceptible to notions that the Mass needs updated to appeal to modern tastes and trending cultural objectives.

At the outset, we have to understand that the liturgy of the Mass is not a *style* of worship, but rather the *action* of worship.[12] It is an action performed publicly by the "whole community" of the Body of Christ,[13] and that action's purpose is this: "the glory of God and the sanctification of the faithful."[14] From start to finish, at every point, the Mass directs our *whole* selves—body and spirit—to Christ, to memorialize and take part in His sacrifice for our salvation. Our *act* of worship is actually our involvement in Christ's sacrifice, for we are offering ourselves (with Christ and through Him) as a sacrifice of thanksgiving and praise to God the Father.[15] This is what St. Paul is talking about: "I appeal to you therefore, brothers and sisters, by the mercies of God, to present your bodies as a living sacrifice, holy and acceptable to God, which is your spiritual worship" (Romans 12:1).[16]

Contrary to commercialized conceptions of religion, we do not participate in the liturgy of the Mass because it is "useful," profiting us in a *utilitarian* way. But rather, it is addition by subtraction; it is our sacrifice of ourselves with Christ that unites us to our Father. As Bishop Robert Barron has said, "The Mass, as an act of union with the highest good, is therefore the supreme instance of play. It is the most useless and hence sublimest activity in which one could possibly engage."[17] And *engaged* we most certainly are, for when we enter into the liturgy we do so in embodied ways that form our desires. "As a being at once body and spirit, man expresses and perceives spiritual realities through physical signs and symbols."[18] All of the embodied rituals of Mass—the introductory Rites (the sign of the cross, the penitential act, etc.), the Liturgy of the Word (Scripture readings, the Responsorial Psalm, standing for the Gospel, the profession of faith, etc.), the Liturgy of the Eucharist (Presentation of the Gifts, the Eucharistic Prayer, the Our Father, receiving of Communion, etc.), and the Concluding Rites—"constitute one single act of worship."[19] In one continuous prayer and offering, through many *physical* signs and symbols, we are joined in Christ with the Church in heaven to God the Father.

The *ultimate* physical signs of our worship—**the sacraments**[20]—are signs that provide us with spiritual grace, and it is in the "visible rites by which the sacraments are celebrated" that the grace is supernaturally conveyed to us.[21] The sacrament of all sacraments is the Eucharist, for all of the other sacraments are "bound up with the Eucharist and are oriented toward it."[22] And just as each sacrament has its own *visible rite* in which the sacrament is received and celebrated (i.e., the baptism rite, the marriage Mass, etc.), so too the Mass is the liturgical celebration that brings us the *sanctifying* grace of the

Eucharist. Moreover, since the Mass is celebrated by the "whole community,"[23] we see that this embodied act of worship is not merely individual, but collective and corporal as well. In fact, the liturgy of the Mass culminates in the *whole* mystical body of Christ consuming the Eucharist—the real body of Christ made present to us. And so, on every occasion of the Mass, we enter into the sacrifice of the *united* Church. As the *Catechism* states:

> "In the Eucharist the sacrifice of Christ becomes also the sacrifice of the members of his Body. The lives of the faithful, their praise, sufferings, prayer, and work, are united with those of Christ and with his total offering, and so acquire a new value. Christ's sacrifice present on the altar makes it possible for all generations of Christians to be united with his offering."[24]

When we corporately celebrate the Eucharistic liturgy and consume the body of Christ, we are involving our personal sacrifice of worship **together** with the worship of others in the most *concrete* practice of our eternal state and remembrance of our eternal home. Is this not the ultimate act of embodied worship? We ingest the *supernatural* Bread of Life, and in so doing we are given the grace to live new lives in this world as ambassadors for the world to come. After we have collectively participated in Christ's redeeming sacrifice of the altar and have received His Eucharistic body, the Mass ("Missa") concludes with us, His mystical body, being sent out on our *mission* to bring Him to the world.[25] This sending out, this remembering and continual recommitment to our mission, cannot happen apart from Christ. The Eucharist is our primary source of sacramental grace as we seek to fulfill our mission on earth and our journey to heaven.

Your Participation in the Mass

Jesus says in John 10:10 that He came to bring us *abundant* life (life to the *full*), and I am convinced that if we approached our worship in the Mass—our entering into the sacrifice of Christ to God the Father—as the most ***real*** thing that we do all week, then we would be living noticeably abundant lives. If we enter Mass each week hungry to receive Christ and offer our lives with His on the altar, then our daily patterns of living would certainly change. We would be less contented here in this world and more eagerly expectant of our heavenly home. As the *Catechism* tells us: "Participation in the Holy Sacrifice identifies us with [Christ's] Heart, sustains our strength along the pilgrimage of this life, makes us long for eternal life, and unites us even now to the Church in heaven, the Blessed Virgin Mary, and all the saints."[26] But to experience this reality, we have to engage ourselves—body and soul—in the worship of the Mass. We should enter into each Mass with intention, with the full knowledge that we are participating—here and now—in the worship of all eternity. We are, in fact, *practicing* our heavenly worship here on earth.

Perhaps that practice is easier said than done if we do not understand the significance of each sign and symbol of the liturgy. Bible scholar Scott Hahn, a former Protestant pastor before coming into the Catholic Church, describes how he discovered that the biblically rooted symbols of the Mass were taken from the book of Revelation:

> …it was only when I began attending Mass that the many parts of this puzzling book suddenly began to fall into place. Before long, I could see the sense in Revelation's altar (Rev. 8:3), its robed clergymen (4:4), candles (1:12), incense (5:8), manna (2:17), chalices (ch. 16), Sunday worship (1:10), the prominence it gives to the Blessed Virgin Mary (12:1–6), the "Holy, Holy, Holy" (4:8), the Gloria (15:3–4), the Sign of the Cross (14:1), the Alleluia (19:1, 3, 6), the readings from Scripture (ch. 2–3), and the "Lamb of God" (many, many times).[27]

While the practice of our faith must be embodied to take root in our hearts and manifest itself in our behaviors, the understanding of faith practices involves our reasoning minds. We have to gain knowledge and search for truth before we can employ that truth to good and beautiful ends. In other words, if we have a poor understanding of the scriptural and traditional basis for the liturgy of the Mass, then we are not able to *fully* enter into its worship. Our minds must be enlightened in order to fully engage our bodies. Consequently, the first step to being able to participate more fully in the Mass is to take the time to educate our minds. I have listed in the section below some helpful resources that serve as a starting point, but do not limit yourself to these. Purpose to develop your understanding of the liturgy. Systematically read through the Church documents and the portions of the *Catechism of the Catholic Church* that speak to the purpose and intended practice of the liturgy.

Secondly, there is intellectual knowledge, and then there is another kind of knowing—*knowing by doing*. In application, it is the idea that we learn to pray by praying; we acquire a full knowledge of reverence by practicing reverent posture; we internalize the words of the creed by saying them over and over, week after week. There is a maxim currently in vogue in popular culture—"fake it 'til you make it." While I think there are some problematic applications of this mindset in the professional world, the effort to practice religious convictions despite lacking full understanding or ideal circumstances is a laudable one, I dare say, even virtuous. There comes a point where we have enough intellectual knowledge, and now we must engage ourselves with it. *We have to jump into the boat.*

What happens when we jump? We might not make graceful landings. We might be uncomfortable. We may find ourselves seasick, travelling through unfamiliar and unexpectedly choppy waters. If the liturgy of the Mass is worship, and worship is *not about us*, then at points we will come face-to-face with the realization that we must throw off some of our old comforts and stylistic preferences. In order to enter into and participate in the Church's liturgical worship, we must conform our practice to its ideals, not the other way around. How do we do this—both as individuals and the Church body as a whole? Once we know the value and importance of a liturgically correct Mass, we will find ourselves obliged to do two things collectively: seek out parishes and individuals dedicated to preserving such an atmosphere of worship; and contribute to reforming our resident parishes that have, over time and through various circumstances, lost essential liturgical elements vital to the celebration of the Mass. It will be hard to practice an embodied faith in a worship environment that has (intentionally or unintentionally) removed many of the signs and symbols that facilitate doing so. If heaven, not earth, is our true home, then our churches' architecture and Masses' liturgies must bear a heavenly resemblance, not an earthly one.

Resources for Embodied Faith

The Lamb's Supper: The Mass as Heaven on Earth, by Scott Hahn

I read this book as a relatively new Catholic, and it revealed to me the substantial scriptural foundation for many of the elements of the liturgy of the Mass. Hahn unites sacred Scripture with church tradition by explaining how the mysteries of the book of Revelation are revealed and symbolized in the celebration of the Mass. He shows how Revelation's images and symbols are central to the elements of the liturgy that brings all of heaven and earth together in worship during every Mass. After reading this book, your experience of Mass will be forever enlightened.

The Wellspring of Worship, by Jean Cordon

This book wonderfully expresses why the Mass is a liturgy of worship from which we should be living out all aspects of our lives. Fr. Cordon divides his discussion of the Mass into three parts: the mystery of the liturgy, the celebration of the liturgy, and the living out of the liturgy. This resource provides a strong foundation for embodied faith in the liturgy of the Mass.

chapter 2

The Sacraments: Embodied Faith in Signs of Grace

*"The purpose of the church is not merely to keep
us safe from the dangers of the world; it is to
bring us to fullness of life.... Wombs are secure,
but they are not our final home; ships are safe,
but they are leading us somewhere."*
—Bishop Robert Barron[28]

Discovering a Sacramental Theology

Bishop Robert Barron, in describing the theological significance and spiritual visions impressed in the architecture of the great cathedrals, has portrayed

Mother Church as analogous to a ship for our journey and a womb for our growth. She is both carrying us home and preparing us for that heavenly destination upon our earthly journey's end. These are beautiful and fitting descriptions of the role that Jesus intended for His Church to play in our lives of faith. The inspired architecture of the glorious churches of medieval Christendom rightly induces a sense of awe; the structure and artistry truly are "embodiments and expressions of Christ" and "constitute a way of seeing, an avenue to another world."[29] Barron's descriptions of the cathedrals' physical designs reveal a *divine intention* for the mystical and institutional Church that many Christians, and even Catholics, have rarely considered: the Church is God's *instrument*[30] for bringing us to heaven.

Before I discovered the Catholic Church and her sacraments, I would have described "church" as an *event* that Christians attended and a *community* to which they belonged. Both the event and the community were, as I was taught, essential elements of my Christian faith. In other words, if you were a Christian (with all that orthodox belief entailed), then you would need both this event and this community to make you a very good one. Perhaps this is not how we young Evangelicals were told to express the significance of church, but I do think this is how we understood it. Good Christians went to church on Sunday morning…and Sunday night…and Wednesday night. However, as I grew through adolescence, college, and young adulthood, I found that many of the peers who once shared such an understanding of and priority for "church" felt its essentialism to morality and a relationship with God less and less. The sentiment—"I don't need a church to have a personal relationship with God"—became commonplace within my generation, as church attendance dwindled among post-evangelicals.

However, as described in the previous chapter, the dispensability of the church *event* and *community* in a Christian's life seemed to lead more and more to an abandonment of orthodoxy altogether. If a relationship with God survived at all, there were no longer any theological parameters for what sort of God that was, and such a relationship certainly seemed anything but "personal." Looking back, I'm unsure whether something lacking in the concept of "church" eventually drew people I knew away from God or whether a diminishing relationship with God caused these individuals to care less about the correct concept of church. Perhaps it was a little of both. Regardless, my struggle and story differed. I never experienced a period of doubting God's existence or questioning whether He cared to have a relationship with me, but I did very much grow to doubt that we had gotten this thing called "church" anywhere close to right. In fact, that is how my husband and I found ourselves taking a hiatus from the event and the community. It's not that we thought them superfluous to our faith; it was that we were growing to suspect that they lacked something essential to our relationship with Christ. Sure enough, we ultimately discovered the essential but missing elements in our experience of the institutional church—the sacraments.

As I have shared, discovering the sacrament of the Eucharist—Christ's mystical body actually present in the bread and wine—was a pivotal point in our family's journey home to the Catholic Church. A religious ritual that we had previously believed to be a mere symbol of Christ's sacrifice turned out to be the primary source of sanctifying grace, which we had lacked access to until that point. We suddenly realized why every expression of the *event* and the *community* of church that we had experienced had not satisfied our longing, nor the longings of others we knew who abandoned the investigation of "church" altogether. The Catholic Church was the only church that was ably to give us Christ's Eucharistic body—to give us not just a symbol but a sacrament, an effectual sign of grace bestowing divine life to us.[31] We quickly discovered the Church's other sacraments as well, other avenues of grace available to us. By this point we were realizing the Church's role as a *sacrament* herself, both containing and distributing her seven particular sacraments to all her members. I saw God's design for His Church and the importance of its sacramental theology, which she had carefully developed over the centuries under the guidance of the Holy Spirit. Before Jesus ascended to the Father,

He saw fit to leave us with a means of accessing His grace and the power of His Spirit while we journey to be with Him. I found that we cannot separate the Church from the sacraments Christ left in her keeping; nor can we separate these sacraments from a relationship with Christ.

Embodied Faith in the Sacraments

When you start to realize that Jesus intended to leave us with a home here on earth—a vessel to carry us and a womb to sustain us—then a sacramental theology makes a whole lot of sense. We don't get to heaven on our own merit or by our own means. We are daily in need of Christ's redemptive work of grace on the cross, and that grace is a *gift*—"the free and underserved help that God gives us to respond to his call to become children of God, adoptive sons, partakers of the divine nature and of eternal life."[32] It is through the Church and her sacraments that we access this grace, for we cannot acquire it for ourselves on our own. As the *Catechism* tells us:

> "The seven sacraments are the signs and instruments by which the Holy Spirit spreads the grace of Christ the head throughout the Church which is his Body. The Church, then, both contains and communicates the invisible grace she signifies. It is in this analogical sense, that the Church is called a 'sacrament.'"[33]

As a *sacrament*, an *instrument* of Christ, the Church's goal in carrying us heavenward involves two ends: to bring us into communion with God and unity with all humanity.[34] Each of the seven sacraments achieve these ends through embodied means in our lives. In other words, they are helping us to keep what Jesus told us were the two great commandments: *love God and love your neighbor*. The story of the Fall is the story of broken relationships—our broken relationship with God and with all of His creatures. The sacraments allow us to live out the narrative of restoration; they bring us into union with God and unity with our brothers and sisters. Through continual streams of grace, each sacrament is accomplishing its own restorative purpose in our spiritual lives.

Baptism

Baptism provides "the sacramental entry into the life of faith,"[35] for it is indeed the "sacrament of faith."[36] We must come to the sacrament through some amount of faith to begin with, which is always a gift. For infants, it is faith on the part of the parents. We have been given the gift of faith within the community of the faithful, but it is not a perfect or mature faith. "For all the baptized, children or adults, faith must grow *after* Baptism."[37] The grace of baptism begins our journey, putting us on the path of salvation. We come into the church marked with the stain of original sin, and we walk out clean. We begin this life of faith by entering into the baptismal promises of fidelity to God, which we renew every Easter.

I take great delight in attending baptisms. Obviously, the baptisms of my own children have been precious moments for me to witness, but I love watching all babies come into the church and receive new life in Christ. The smell of the sacred chrism, the symbol of the white garment across their chests, the lighting of their candles—these are all powerful signifiers of what is taking place at that moment in a child's soul. That child of God is being claimed for Christ. The essential part of the baptism rite—the immersion in or pouring on the head of the holy water in name of the Father, Son, and Holy Spirit—"signifies and actually brings about death to sin and entry into the life of the Most Holy Trinity through configuration to the Paschal mystery of Christ."[38]

The imagery and symbolism the Church gives us in baptism is profound. Once the sacrament has been received, the candle—the "light of faith"—is then lit. It is lit from the Easter candle, signifying the source of that child's new life in the sacrifice of Christ—what we celebrate every Sunday and especially at Easter. Baptism ignites that light, starting us on our journey home to heaven; and we are to keep our lamps burning strong, to grow our faith (particularly through all of the other sacraments) until our earthly pilgrimages come to an end. A couple of years ago I attended a funeral in close succession to a baptism, and it was the first Catholic funeral I ever remember attending. When I saw the Easter candle lit at the front, tears filled my eyes; for I realized at that moment the bookends of this Catholic's life. This person's journey had come to an end, and it had ended where it had begun—at the altar of faith. The same Paschal lamp that lit the baby girl's baptism candle so many years before stood burning by the old woman's coffin. Through Christ's Church, this woman had been reborn into His life; through His Church she had lived that life of faith; and now too, that same Church was witnessing her passage into eternal life with Him.

Confirmation

As with Baptism, there is a tendency for Catholics to view Confirmation as this one-time event, this box to check. After all, you don't receive these sacraments continually as you do with the Eucharist, and we can easily come to think of them as *events in the past*. But we are making a consequential mistake when we take the view that the grace of Confirmation is merely a singular, rite-of-passage event of our youth. If this is our mindset, then we will fail to live out of the grace stores that have been planted within our souls during this sacrament. After Baptism and the Eucharist, Confirmation is the final of the three "sacraments of initiation."[39] Confirmation "deepens" and "perfects" baptismal grace,[40] and during the sacrament the individual fittingly renews the baptismal promises. Just as Baptism takes away a mark (the stain of sin) and marks us for Christ, Confirmation applies its own mark—the indelible "seal" of the Holy Spirit on a person's soul.[41]

When I think of being sealed with the mark of the Holy Spirit, I love to envision those beautiful, red wax seals of the past that bore the imprint of official insignia. Such a seal *authorizes* a document, and in the sacrament of Confirmation we are being authorized with vital spiritual power from that moment forward. It anchors us more deeply in the life and love of the Holy Trinity: making us respond to the divine love of our Father, uniting us more steadfastly to Christ, and increasing the gifts of the Holy Spirit in our lives. In addition, this sacrament strengthens our bond with Christ's Church and provides us with the power of the Spirit "to spread and defend the faith by word and action as true witnesses of Christ, to confess the name of Christ boldly, and never to be ashamed of the Cross."[42] Picture that image of the red wax seal again. That's what is indelibly written in it at Confirmation. That's the *power* that has been imprinted on your soul as you journey toward heaven.

Eucharist

In the last chapter about the Mass I mentioned that the Eucharist is the "sacrament of sacraments," for it is actually the mystical body of Christ that is being consumed by the physical body of Christ. It is, therefore, powerfully accomplishing the end goal of all the sacraments—*to unify us with God and His Church*—as often as we take it. For a Catholic to live an embodied faith, there is no getting around the fact that frequently receiving the Eucharist—therefore frequently participating in Mass—is vital.[43] You won't be able to find one canonized saint in the Church who wasn't passionate about receiving the Eucharist as often as possible. Our Church and her priests bring us Jesus at *every* Mass, multiple times a day, all around the world. We in the Western world live during a time of incredible access to this sacrament, yet we take it so much for granted. I know that I take it for granted. *Jesus, forgive us for not realizing the gift that is so readily available to us, and help us to practice devotion to You in this blessed sacrament.*

Penance

If we are to be receiving our Lord in the Eucharist frequently, then the state of our souls is something that needs to be regularly assessed. St. Paul reminds us to examine our consciences before partaking in the sacrament:

> "Whoever, therefore, eats the bread or drinks
> the cup of the Lord in an unworthy manner will
> be guilty of profaning the body and blood of the
> Lord. Let a man examine himself, and so eat
> the bread and drink of the cup. For anyone who

> eats and drinks without discerning the body
> eats and drinks judgment upon himself."[44]

If we are partaking of the Eucharist frequently, then we will quickly become aware of our need for frequently receiving the sacrament of penance as well. While the Penance is required for removing *mortal* sin before receiving the body of Christ, the more frequent removal of *venial* sins becomes a balm to our souls and opens up wide channels of grace to hear the Holy Spirit speak to our hearts continually. Also called the sacrament of "Reconciliation," this sacrament is working in a particular way in all baptized persons, to restore our broken relationships—both with God and others.[45] Baptism takes away the otherwise fixed stain of original sin, being "the first and chief sacrament of the forgiveness of sins;"[46] and Penance then forgives us of our sins thereafter. We should take great comfort in the fact that "[t]here is no offense, however, serious, that the Church cannot forgive," and that through this sacrament of His Church, Christ intends that "the gates of forgiveness should always be open to anyone who turns away from sin."[47]

Remember that white garment we received at Baptism? Mother Mary Loyola gives a beautiful image of the role the sacrament of Reconciliation plays in keeping your white garment clean in her classic children's allegory, *The King of the Golden City*:

"So [the King] was not content that the exiles should be his servants and subjects only. He wished to adopt them and make them his children, most dear children, whilst they were quite tiny. When this was done, a beautiful white robe called "Grace" was given them, and their names were written in a book called "The Book of Life." No one could take the robe from them, or blot their names out of that Book—no one *but themselves*."[48]

Mother Loyola continues the metaphor later on by describing the white robe's necessity in coming to the King's "banquet hall" and "banquet table":

"One thing only [the King] strictly required of all—the white robe. No one might come to his table without it, under pain of incurring his displeasure and dreadful punishment... Near the hall was an ante-chamber where a white robe might be had by all who applied for it properly. Small stains on the robe did not prevent people from sitting down at the table. Still, the purer it was, the more welcome was the wearer, and the richer were the jewels with which the King was sure to adorn it. So the guests were advised to remove all spots as far as possible."[49]

We have been given a royal, white robe of "Grace," and we have been blessed with the means of retaining its luminescence. Why would we walk around with spots on it? Why do we go so long between washings? Are we not concerned to be wearing a soiled garment to the King's banquet table? The examples of the saints would point us to the practice of regular and frequent confession and reconciliation. Let us be quick to partake of the sacrament offered to us while in exile, and practice maintaining the robe's whiteness, which will be ever white in our heavenly home.

Anointing of the Sick

There is a trend among secular scholars who study the historical figure of Jesus in the Gospel narratives to downplay or entirely overlook what made up most of Jesus' earthly ministry—miracles of healing. You can hardly go a chapter without a blind person regaining sight, a lame man walking, a hemorrhaging woman cured, or a child being raised from the dead. I suppose if we are on a campaign to demystify the Christian faith, then glossing over Jesus' record of healing is a good place to start. All of the sacraments reignite the supernatural in our lives, but one particular sacrament—the Anointing of the Sick—maintains our faith in Christ's healing power. The Church carries on the work of healing the sick, as Christ appointed the apostles to do while He walked with them.[50]

Priests administer this sacrament to anyone with a "serious illness" by anointing the forehead and hands with blessed oil and praying the following over the believer: "Through this holy anointing may the Lord in his love and mercy help you with the grace of the Holy Spirit. May the Lord who frees you from sin save you and raise you up."[51]

God doesn't heal the physical needs of every person who receives this sacrament, nor every person who simply prays for healing. We won't know *why* on this side of heaven. There is much mystery to sickness and suffering in this life that Mother Church does not resolve for us with clear-cut answers and formulas. However, the Church recognizes an important connection between sickness of the body and sickness of the soul. *Physical healing is always leading to spiritual healing.* When Jesus healed people, He often did it in the same breath with which He forgave their sins:

> "Which is easier, to say to the paralytic, 'Your sins are forgiven,' or to say, 'Stand up and take your mat and walk'? But so that you may know that the Son of Man has authority on earth to forgive sins"—[Jesus] said to the paralytic— "I say to you, stand up, take your mat and go to your home." (Matthew 9:5-6)

The reason physical healing and miracles are so powerful is that they provide us with physical signs of the greater healing He is capable of doing, and *is* doing, in our souls. Yes, it is life changing and physically relieving for someone to be cured of pain or healed from a debilitating illness; but the existence of supernatural healing is evidence of the existence of an almighty God who loves us at work in our lives. The event of healing in our bodies is but a taste of what awaits us and will be our eternal state.

Holy Orders

It was remarkable for me to discover the unbroken apostolic succession of Catholic bishops all the way back to the first twelve apostles and the first pope, Peter.[52] In instituting Peter as the head of His Church, Christ gave His Church the hierarchical leadership to guide and preserve His mission for her throughout the ages. This sacrament gives us our priests, who—*in persona Christi*[53]—bring us Jesus Himself in the Mass. They are quite literally bringing salvation to the world in the primary role of their calling[54] or *vocation*:

> "…acting in the person of Christ and proclaiming his mystery, they unite the votive offerings of the faithful to the sacrifice of Christ their head, and in the sacrifice of the Mass they make present again and apply, until the coming of the Lord, the unique sacrifice of the New Testament, that namely of Christ

> offering himself once for all a spotless victim
> to the Father." From this unique sacrifice their
> whole priestly ministry draws its strength.[55]

It is profoundly beautiful that in strengthening the rest of the faithful in offering the Mass, priests are also strengthening themselves for all of the duties of their lives and vocations. We see echoed in this sacrament the centrality of the Mass and the Eucharist to our faith. These sacraments are intertwined. We need the priest to celebrate the Mass, which brings us Jesus' Eucharistic body. The grace from this sacrament flows through the priestly vocation and offering out to all the body of Christ, sustaining us in this world and preparing us for the ultimate banquet feast with Christ in heaven.

Matrimony

I wasn't aware at the time, but looking back, I realize that my marriage was the *main* avenue God used to bring me into the Catholic Church. I have often thought that had it not been for my husband, Mike, I may never have become Catholic; without his honest investigation of truth and response to the Holy Spirit's leading, I may never have experienced the graces that have flooded my life since coming home to the Church. While I was seeking truth and seeking God's will individually, my marriage and my spouse were aligning me with God's ultimate will for my life. *I was living sacramentally*; I just didn't know it yet.

With every year of marriage, I reflect back and realize how much of myself has been sanctified through this sacrament, as well as how much still deeply needs to be sanctified. I see the fruit that comes from two people struggling together to allow the Holy Spirit to use each one to make the other holy, to help the other become a saint. My husband is the best mirror I have for revealing my sinful flaws and selfish inclinations. Quite honestly, without him in my life, there would be many faults I could *easily* ignore. If you are married, you know exactly what I mean. Our spouses see the ugly part of ourselves that we effectively keep hidden from everyone else; but our spouses also see the depth and beauty of our hearts that gradually become known in the life of a marriage. Each in their own shortcomings, husband and wife reveal the other's deepest brokenness that needs restored and provide opportunities for each person to *practice* holiness. It's a *privileged* position; and it is a sacramental relationship that is meant to signify Christ's relationship with and love for His bride, the Church. Our *Catechism* expounds this truth so perfectly:

> This grace proper to the sacrament of Matrimony is intended to perfect the couple's love and to strengthen their indissoluble unity.

> By this grace they "help one another to attain holiness in their married life and in welcoming and educating their children."

> *Christ is the source of this grace...* Christ dwells with them, gives them the strength to take up their crosses and so follow him, to rise again after they have fallen, to forgive one another, to bear one another's burdens, to "be subject to one another out of reverence for Christ," and to love one another with supernatural, tender, and fruitful love.[56]

If we let the full weight of this realization wash over us, would we not approach our marriages differently? If this bond of grace, this signification of Christ and His Church, is what God joined at the altar when we made our wedding vows before Him, then do we not need to practice a different vision of ourselves and our spouses in our marriages? Should we not view being charged with the body and soul of another, "to have and to hold" and to help get to heaven, as the most privileged of positions? But so often we fall into the consumeristic and utilitarian perspectives of marriage. It often becomes a status symbol or an accessory to our lives that must fulfill the expectations we placed on it from the outset. We miss all of the grace and the sacramental reality of it when we choose to live out of that mindset, and such a mindset will never sustain the marriage of two broken people on the journey toward restoration.

There is a wonderful grace God gives in the gift of a spouse, because our spouses do not need to be perfect to help reveal our flaws and point us toward redemption. It is actually their defects and our recoiling at those faults that offer us the best opportunities to examine our own consciences. As with all of the seven sacraments, our marriages in the Church are instruments that make us fit for heaven, if we let them.

Celebrating and Receiving the Graces

Peter Kreeft has said, "Sacraments are like hoses. They are the channels of the living water of God's grace. Our faith is like opening the faucet. We can open it a lot, a little, or not at all."[57] What do we want? Do we want to live with a little trickle of grace, or do we want to be carried away in a flood? The answer should be obvious, but perhaps it's a truth we tend to forget. Just like the Israelites in the Bible, we forget God's faithfulness and provision for our lives. We wander around in circles looking for help in this life and forget that we have been given *riches of grace* in the Church's sacraments. "His divine power has given us everything needed for life and godliness."[58] We just need to receive those gifts continually. I believe *receiving* in an embodied life of faith is closely connected to *celebrating*. We rightly say the priest "celebrates" the Mass, for there is rejoicing and thanksgiving involved in the offering of the sacrifice to the Father and then again in our own reception of that sacrifice. The embodied act of *celebration*—of thanksgiving and rejoicing—helps us receive the graces in all of the sacraments.

We should continually *celebrate* the new life of Baptism, the seal of the Holy Spirit at Confirmation, the presence of Christ in the Eucharist, the freedom from sin in Penance, the power of Christ's healing touch on our bodies and souls in the Anointing of the Sick, and the sacramental vocations—whether Holy Orders or Matrimony—that offer us a particular pathway of holiness on the road to heaven. These celebrations can take many different forms. My family loves to celebrate "Baptism days" the way we celebrate birthdays, and the kids *quickly* pick up on the significance. Imagine if we all got *two* birthday celebrations every year, two cakes, two days where those we love celebrated our lives. Celebrating Baptism days is a beautiful way to keep the gift of new life in Christ's Church a reality that our children (and we) remain conscious of throughout our lives. None of our children have reached the age of Confirmation yet, but our family celebrates the anniversary of Mike and me being Confirmed and our family coming into the Church; it's like a second anniversary for us. I have heard of parents taking their children on special one-on-one Confirmation trips to whatever destination the child chooses. The travel lover in me likes that idea of a celebration a lot.

We can celebrate the gift of the Mass and the Eucharist with young children by doing something special (like going for doughnuts) together right after. We can carve out special alone time with the Eucharist in Adoration on a day or evening that is part of our free time or part of a date with our spouses. We can regularly read the recorded miracles of the Eucharist or about miraculous healings that have taken place in those who have received the Anointing of the Sick, combining our own thanksgiving with that person's by acknowledging God's healing power in the sacraments. There are many ways to practice celebrating the gifts of the sacraments in our lives. But whatever particular form the celebrating takes, the point is that the act of celebration is keeping our lives anchored in the vital grace of the sacraments. The more we practice being thankful for grace the more we will remember to partake of it.

Resources for Embodied Faith
The Seven Sacraments: Entering the Mysteries of God, by Stratford Caldecott

This book brings our attention to the important mysteries that we find hidden in the sacraments, mysteries that are missing from modern approaches to the sacramental life of the Church. This book will bring a fresh spiritual and scriptural approach to the sacraments of the Church, as Caldecott unpacks the power and symbolism contained in each one.

The Word, Church, and Sacraments: in Protestantism and Catholicism, by Louis Bouyer

This short book offers a concise comparison of the differences between Protestant and Catholic conceptions of three things: the Word of God, the authority of the Church, and the sacraments. The whole book is helpful, particularly for those seeking to understand important differences between Protestant and Catholic beliefs; but it is the last section on the sacraments that addresses what I've discussed in this chapter.

chapter 3

The Domestic Church: Embodied Faith in Family Life

"The history of mankind, the history of salvation
passes by way of the family... The family
is placed at the center of the great struggle
between good and evil, between life and death,
between love and all that is opposed to love."
—St. Pope John Paul II, Familiaris Consortio

Discovering the Domestic Church

It was summer 2011, and Mike and I had been struggling with questions of what church and worship were intended to be. As we considered various conflicts we had with our Evangelical backgrounds and, more and more, with Protestantism as a whole, we found ourselves looking back into history and starting to bump into Catholicism. But neither of us had really been exposed to families that were *practicing* Catholics. We knew quite a few Evangelical Christians who grew up Catholic, but they had left the Catholic Church and experienced a personal faith in Christ elsewhere. So the idea of considering Catholicism was not at all on our radar.

We were also new parents. Our oldest son, Tyler, had been born that April, and he completely changed our world. We were suddenly a family of three; it was not just the two of us anymore. We knew God had blessed us with the best gift in the world, but with that joyful realization we also felt the full weight of our responsibility as Christian parents. Not only were we given this little life for which to nourish and care, we also had been entrusted with a *soul*, and with a significant role in that soul's spiritual formation and journey to heaven. If we weren't even sure what the Church was supposed to look like or the ultimate purpose of Sunday worship, how were we going to know how to be the best Christian parents we could? Of course we had grown up with some good examples of Christian parents, our parents among them; but we had also grown up with plenty of fellow youth group friends who no longer identified themselves as Christians. We believed our child had been given a free will with which to choose faith in Christ for himself, but we wanted our expression of faith in our family to be something he never considered a stumbling block to that choice. And with these desires in our hearts and on our minds, we bumped into Catholicism again—but this time not on paper. We met two Catholic families.

My husband, a literature teacher at the time at DeMatha Catholic High School, had become good friends with a fellow teacher, Matt Fish. Matt had been teaching theology at the school for a couple of years, but he had discerned the call to the priesthood and would be leaving at the end of the summer to enter seminary in Rome for the next four years. Matt and my husband had already had numerous conversations about the Catholic faith. Matt's Catholic background had been different from that of other Catholics we had met. He grew up in a devout family, and his father was a deacon in the Church. He had attended college at Franciscan University of Steubenville in Ohio, where he came away with both a faith-filled undergraduate experience and lifelong Catholic friends, many of whom ended up settling in or around the Washington, DC area. In fact, Matt had been telling us for a while about two particular families in the area—the Nortons and the Pollocks—whom we "just had to meet." That summer an opportunity came. Nate and Candace Pollock were hosting a farewell dinner for Matt at their home, along with Matt and Mary Norton, and they invited us to join them. It was kind of unusual to be invited to dinner by folks you had never met, especially since this was a special dinner for their good friend before he left the country for a few years. Mike and I are very social, and we love meeting new people; but, having not interacted with many Catholic families (especially those with young children like us), we had no idea what to expect.

As soon as we walked through their front door, the spirit of hospitality was an overwhelming presence. Sometimes you meet people and just instantly know there is something special about them; you might not know what it is at that moment, but it wraps you up like a warm blanket. Christ's presence in their home and lives brought an instant ecumenical spirit and common bond to our fellowship. We felt so welcomed, and all the kids (they each had four at the time) were excited that we had a little baby! We gathered around the table, prayed a collective "Bless us, O, Lord," and enjoyed a delicious home-cooked Southern meal. We got to hear about a lot of their shared college experiences at Steubenville, and we were excited to find out more about a college that was producing such "evangelical" Catholic young adults with a charismatic faith. I felt the presence of the Holy Spirit in the expression of their Catholicism. *There is something here*, I thought; whatever we had just stepped into was something very *good* and full of *beauty*, something I couldn't help but want in the fabric of our family culture. There was an aesthetic you couldn't miss. It was distinctly Catholic—not in an overpowering way—but in a way that simply touched every element and person. Their children were delightful; both the little ones and the older ones were filled with joy and wonder, qualities that seem to wear off young children too quickly in our modern culture. Until that night, I had no reference point for what a Catholic family looked like; after being in their home, I wanted that same spirit and culture in our growing family.

As we talked throughout the evening, particularly as I visited with Mary and Candace, my heart started filling with the sense of *home*. It was sort of like that feeling you get when you have been away from where you came from for a long time and come back, or that excitement you get making your return from a long trip and the road signs and landmarks start looking familiar again; you know you are getting close. I had been following Christ my whole life. I had been a Christian as long as I could remember; but in my post-marriage adult years, as we were searching through faith traditions, I felt more like I was a Christian on a journey, a Christian without a home. That night I think I had my first sense of coming home, but to a home I had never known. Getting in the car to leave, my eyes teared up. I told Mike that it had been a long time since my heart had had that feeling; something was being stirred up inside of me. At that moment, I may not have been any closer to knowing what Sunday morning worship should look like or whether we would convert to Catholicism, but I suddenly had a clearer vision for our Christian faith in our home as our children grew up.

I didn't know at the time, because I hadn't yet been introduced to the concept; but what I was sensing and perceiving, that beautiful presence drawing me in at the Pollocks' home, was the *domestic church*—the expression of the body of Christ in the family. A vibrant domestic church can transform the culture around it; its goodness is contagious. The *Catechism* teaches us that "believing families are of primary importance as centers of living, radiant faith…" The domestic church of the family is where each member "learns endurance and the joy of work, fraternal love, generous—even repeated— forgiveness, and above all divine worship in prayer and the offering of one's life."[59] As Mike and I have begun to cultivate our domestic church—*our* "center of living and radiant faith" for ourselves and our now four children—I am so thankful for the gift of faithful Catholic families who have been an inspiration to us. They exude love, joy, forgiveness, devotion to prayer, and self-sacrifice.

My hope and prayer continue to be that my own domestic church compels hearts, and that when people step into the life of my family they would be wrapped in the love of Christ and of His Church. We had just had our second son, Walker, when we entered the Church and baptized our two boys on June 22, 2013. Matt and

Mary became Ty's godparents and Candace and Nate became Walker's. Fr. Matt, ordained a Washington, DC Archdiocese priest in the summer of 2015, is godfather to our third son, Sam. It seems so appropriate that the vocations that first inspired the birth of our own domestic church would have a permanent place in our family as the godparents of our children. In a very real sense, we found the universal Catholic Church through her presence in the domestic church.

Embodied Faith in the Domestic Church

I grew up learning a good deal about Christian apologetics and how to make a compelling argument to an outsider for my Christian faith. Apologetics has it place; but truth is most compelling when we see it lived out in a life. I believe there is nothing that compels people toward Catholicism more than encountering authentic Catholic families. Take that thought a step further: there is nothing that compels children and young adults to make their Catholic faith their own more than growing up within an authentic Catholic family. The domestic church is a *living apologetic* because it is the essence of embodied faith. When people witness the Church's sacraments, liturgy, and traditions embodied in the daily faith ritual and narrative of committed Catholics, they cannot help getting caught up in that story—whether they are children growing up inside it or others looking in from the outside.

When my husband and I were investigating the Catholic faith, we found much of the theology logically consistent, and the Church's teachings seemed to resolve many tensions or questions we were struggling with from our Evangelical background. But these theological arguments alone did not bring us the whole way. In our journey to Catholicism we hit a point of no return when we encountered families that were *living* their Catholicism. While it is important to understand the truth of our Catholic faith and be able to articulate it intelligently, this reasoned knowledge is mostly aimed at convincing the mind. As we have discussed at the outset, if truth is to *change who we are*, it has to hit the formational realm of our desiring hearts. Truth hits the target of a person's heart when it is made real through the life of another. If our goal—our target—is to lead souls to the Church, then intellectual knowledge of our faith is the bow, not the arrow. People are the arrows; and the quiver of the Church needs to be full of well-formed arrows.

As parents, we can intuitively see how we are not just raising "thinking beings"; we are first and foremost raising "desiring beings." In fact, when raising little ones, we can't help but deal with desire *first*. Our children don't hit the age of reason until about age seven, but we don't wait to teach them right and wrong until then. Though they can't think rationally about morality at a very young age, that doesn't mean they aren't learning to be moral during that time. As parents, we are helping them form virtue through practice and the imitation of our lives. Before we teach their minds what it means to desire God, we are teaching them to actually *practice* desiring Him. Our family home and life is where this practice primarily takes place. Our children are able to worship with us in Mass on Sunday, because they have practiced worship at home with us. What they participate in at church at the end of the week mirrors and culminates their experiences throughout the week in family life.

The *Catechism* describes this primary role of the family clearly: "The Christian home is the place where children receive the first proclamation of the faith. For this reason, the family home is rightly called 'the domestic church,' a community of grace and prayer, a school of human virtues and of Christian charity."[60] The domestic church is ultimately a school of *charity*—love. Our homes and family lives are where each person within is to learn to *love* God. How do we do this, though? How does the domestic church form this desire and fulfill this role? We can answer these questions by revealing what the domestic church is meant to be.

It's a **Sign** of God's Love

The domestic church is a powerful sign, both to members of the family and to those outside, because it depicts in its structure and divine design the love of our Triune God:

"The Christian family is a communion of persons, a sign and image of the communion of the Father and the Son in the Holy Spirit. In the procreation and education of children it reflects the Father's work of creation."[61] God the Father is the Lover, and God the Son is the Beloved, and the communion they share in the Holy Spirit is *Love*. Now take the family as a sign of that love. You have the father and the mother—the *lover* and the *beloved*—and their communion together produces *love* in the expression of children. By God's beautiful design, the family is meant to be a picture of ultimate love—divine love.

Moreover, the family "has an evangelizing and missionary task."[62] That means that our expression of family life should remind people of God's love. Yes, it's a tall order, a hard goal. We will fail at it many times, but we must keep striving for it. We need our children and our world to see God's love for *them*. Experiencing His desire for them is what compels them to desire Him in return.

It's an Education in Prayer

Your children may learn prayers in church, but they won't develop lives of prayer from attending weekend Mass or CCD classes. They will learn what prayer is from your family's prayer life and habits. "The *Christian family* is the first place of education in prayer," the *Catechism* teaches us. "Based on the sacrament of marriage, the family is the 'domestic church' where

God's children learn to pray 'as the Church' and to persevere in prayer."[63] For the domestic church to help form a desire for God in its members, it will have to be a family that prays together—through the good times and through the hard times. In their formation, our children are witnesses of our individual faithfulness in prayer, but they are also participants in the prayer life of the family and the greater Church.

Praying together as a family is probably the most important activity of the domestic church, because children learn to pray by praying; and these times of prayer provide vital nourishment for their little desiring hearts. "For young children in particular, daily family prayer is the first witness of the Church's living memory as awakened patiently by the Holy Spirit."[64] The light of Christ, the Holy Spirit, is given to our children at their baptisms, and this is a flame that we want to keep burning brightly. Prayer is fuel for that flame and opens each member of our families to the move of the Holy Spirit in their lives.

It's a **Preparation** *for Adult Life*

Childhood in the domestic church is both a playground and a practice field. It is a space to discover wonder for the world and its Creator by being introduced to truth, beauty, and goodness. It is also a space where individuals learn to become virtuous people. As the Church rightly teaches, the family is *the* building block of society:

> "The family is the *original cell of social life*. It is the natural society in which husband and wife are called to give themselves in love and in the gift of life. Authority, stability, and a life of relationships within the family constitute the foundations for freedom, security, and fraternity within society. The family is the community in which, from childhood, one can learn moral values, begin to honor God, and make good use of freedom. Family life is an initiation into life in society."[65]

Ultimately, if we don't have virtuous families, we won't have virtuous societies. We practice love for both God and our fellow man within our families; and in this context, virtue takes root. Self-giving is formed through sibling interactions or through the generous efforts of a parent with a needy little one. Respect for authority is nurtured within a loving hierarchy of the parent-child dynamic. Patience and love are imparted through many "teachers" and countless opportunities in this school of virtue. When one has grown up within a domestic church, in the form it should be, that individual will be prepared to live as a faith-filled adult, bringing truth, beauty, and goodness to society at large.

There is a difference in growing up "Catholic" and growing up in a *domestic church*. I am convinced that many situations of individuals leaving the Catholic faith are a direct result of the faith not being alive in their homes. The truth taught in Sunday Mass, in First Communion preparation, and in Confirmation classes was not embodied in the daily rituals and narrative of their family life. The Catholic home is the heart of faith for our families because it is where our hearts' desire is formed: where we witness the powerful image of God's love for us, where we practice talking to Him and hearing His voice, and where we grow in virtue so we can bring God's love to a world that needs it.

The Domestic Church in Your Home

The first step in making your home a domestic church is realizing that **it is one**. Your marriage is a sacrament, and your family is a domestic church. As with much of our faith, we have to simply begin to take part in the reality that is. Since the life of your family *is* a **sign**, an **education in prayer**, and a **formation in individual virtue**, then we need to examine the substance that's there. *In what ways is my family a sign of God's love—to those within and those outside it? What opportunities do the members of my family have to learn prayer? How are the rhythms of family life developing virtue in everyone—from the littlest all the way up to Mom and Dad?* Reflecting on these questions will spark a flame in your domestic church to become the kind of home the

Catholic Church teaches us to be. But how do we fuel that fire and keep the light of our families burning brightly?

In Catholic spirituality there is *unity* without *uniformity*. Catholicism embraces the beautiful diversity of unique individuals and families; and Church teaching helps us differentiate between the universal *substance and purpose* of the family and the *expression* of each domestic church, which is its own unique thread in the tapestry of the greater Church. Your domestic church is not to be compared to that of your friends or others in your parish (or on social media). Your domestic church is not your branded and stylized Catholic faith; it is your family's faithful and authentic expression of Catholicism in your daily living. It will look different from the lives of other Catholic families, and that is good. What should be common to all are the things the Church teaches are central to the role of the family. In that regard, I would offer some guiding principles for your domestic church:

Firstly, realize that **the Catholic home is the primary school, and parents are the primary teachers.** Whether your kids go to public school, Catholic school, private school, are homeschooled, attend CCD, or go to youth group—never forget that their primary school for life and faith is their family, and their primary teachers are you, their parents. So, cultivate homes with a life-giving atmosphere, and be the kinds of individuals you want your children to imitate. If you want your children to follow

Christ, regularly ask yourself how much you look like Him. In addition to you, there are many role models and other teachers that will help form your children's desires and instill virtues in them, but they are at *your* service. In light of this fact, we as parents should be discerning about the individuals and institutions we allow to participate in our children's formation.

Secondly, **practice praying as a family.** The prayer life of your domestic church may look very different than the prayer life of another Catholic family. Maybe you start your day with Morning Prayer; or you may pray the rosary together after dinner. Perhaps praying as a family begins with cuddling up at bedtime and reciting the Our Father, listing intentions, and thanking God for His goodness and grace that day. Your family prayer life will be dynamic, not static; it will grow and take new shape over time, especially as you move through different seasons of family life. The exact prayers and timing of them is *not* what is most important; what is of primary worth is that you are lifting your hearts to heaven together, that you are daily acknowledging the Source of life within your home.

Thirdly, **be a home of servants and a family that serves**. If our domestic churches are to be signs of God's love and their members resemble Jesus, then we must be servants and practice serving. We should be serving each other within our home and serving those with needs (physical and spiritual) outside of it. This means opening up time for service and cultivating rhythms of service in our daily, weekly, monthly, and yearly lives. I have friends who, with their children, volunteer with local community ministries one morning a week. I know countless people who make meals on a regular basis, their children alongside, for individuals within their parish who just had a baby or have been in the hospital. There are others I know who volunteer as a family (young and old) every Christmas season at a soup kitchen. In addition to serving those in need and their communities, families can practice being in the service of each other. Daily life together allows for many opportunities to serve: reading a book to a younger sibling, helping tidy toys or set the table, giving someone else the last cookie, or slipping an encouraging note in someone's lunch box. The thriving domestic church teaches love through serving and joy in service.

As you begin to cultivate the unique expression of your family's faith life, remember that the Holy Spirit is your ultimate guide. He is the light that keeps our home fires burning, and His presence is the life-giving breath of our domestic churches. There are limitless ways for families to serve, pray, and pass on the faith together. Through these corporate and formational faith-embodied activities of the domestic church, each person acquires a deeper desire for God. The Baltimore *Catechism* asks the question: "Why did God make you?" The answer: "God made me to know Him, to love Him, and to serve Him, in this world and to be happy with Him forever in the next." This is what we are doing as the domestic church; we are journeying to heaven, *together*.

Resources for Embodied Faith

We and Our Children: How to Make a Catholic Home, by Mary Reed Newland

Given that this book was originally published in 1954, some of the language, style, and cultural references might be out of vogue. However, she covers a wide range of important matters of the domestic church, and she articulates them beautifully. The book starts from the premise that parents are the primary educators of their children, and Newland addresses the important areas of education and formation that should happen in the home, including: knowledge of God, how to pray, detachment to the world, the Mass, purity, death and dying, the sacraments, the purpose of the liturgical year, and the purpose of work and play. Many of her methods of introducing these topics to children and her wise insights make this a timeless resource for parents.

The Little Oratory: A Beginner's Guide to Praying in the Home, by David Clayton and Leila Lawler

This is a beautiful book that offers something for every domestic Church, whether families have been praying together for a while or are trying to get started. This book is about more than just the prayers we pray in the home; it emphasizes the ways in which we can create atmospheres of prayer in our homes, spaces that cultivate embodied practices for our domestic churches. Clayton and Lawler walk readers through how to set up a "little Oratory" or prayer corner in their homes; and they explain how intentional placement of sacred images and icons helps to create a truly prayerful and Catholic atmosphere. There are beautiful sketches throughout and prints from the author in the back of the book that can be removed for framing. We have a couple of these sacred images hanging above our prayer table.

chapter 4

The Liturgical Year: Embodied Faith in the Rhythms of Daily Life

"At each period in the liturgical Cycle, my missal and Breviary disclose to me new rays of the love of Him Who is for us at the same time Teacher, Doctor, Consoler, Savior, and Friend."
—*Jean-Baptist Chautard*

Discovering the Liturgical Year

I *love* Christmastime. I did as a kid, and I love it even more now as a mom. I remember my childhood anticipation of the bonanza of gifts to be opened Christmas morning. Christmas was all any kid could think of for a good two months before the day actually came, as the sights and sounds pointed to the promise of toys and parties and endless reindeer and Santa-shaped treats. As a kid, I didn't mind that earlier and earlier every year, almost as soon as Halloween candy aisles had been cleared, the red and green and sparkling tinsel filled up supermarket shelves and department store displays.

However, in my post-college years and first few years of marriage I became really bothered by how early decorations went up at stores. I noticed how much "Christmas cheer" was connected to material goods and how quickly those goods became passé. *The iPod you got for Christmas last year is now ancient—no worries—a new one will be released in time for Black Friday...and Cyber Monday.* I found less emphasis placed on permanent pieces of tradition. Instead of inheriting Grandma's china and tree ornaments, you could buy ones that *looked just like them* at Urban Outfitters (albeit "Made in China" and won't last three generations). More and more "disposable" décor and entertaining paraphernalia were everywhere. Magazine covers reinforced the concept of *newness* to holiday celebrations with "this year's best recipes" and "ten ideas for your tree theme." It was everywhere—this colossal, materialistic buildup to December 25, and it had *nothing* to do with Christmas. But that is not the part that really bothered me; after all, there has always been a secular festivity to Christmas in our society.

What concerned me was that my religious Christmas aesthetic was not *distinct*. In fact, it seemed to me that we Christians prepared for and anticipated Christmas in ways that looked *very* similar to the consumerist narrative I saw in the shopping malls and magazine stands. It seemed that without a distinct aesthetic and tradition of its own, the Christian celebration of Christmas had become lost among alternate traditions and aesthetics that were prominent and easily absorbed. The strongest indication of this cultural and ritualistic absorption was that the holiday ended abruptly on December 26. As soon as the "return" stations went up in department stores and the decorations went out of window displays, Christmas was over. When the Christmas tree in the mall came down, so did the one in our living room. Was it coincidence that Christians stopped celebrating Christ's birthday immediately after the last present could be purchased; or could it be that our conception of the parameters of our Christian holiday had somewhere stepped in sync with the rhythms of the consumerist Christmas narrative?

This was troubling for me. Why was the overall form and fashion of our Christmas celebration muffled with the secular holiday? There seemed to be no distinctly Christian *ritual* of Christmas within Christian culture, at least not within the Christian culture in which I grew up. Don't get me wrong—I heard many Sunday sermons on the dangers of materialism and "don't take Christ out of Christmas"; and of course the churches we attended, and my parents, emphasized that Christ's birth was the "reason for the season"—but the fact still remained that our holiday looked more similar to secular culture's version of Christmas than distinct from it. I couldn't quite piece it together at the time, but after becoming Catholic I realized that these inklings about the lack of distinctly Christian ritual in our Christian holidays point to realities that extended far beyond Christmas.

I didn't really understand liturgical living when we entered the Church in June 2013. I hadn't fully processed the liturgy beyond the Sunday mass; I was still trying to nail down all my participation parts, sometimes resorting to lip reading along with the priest if there wasn't a card in the pew. As our first Christmas as Catholics approached, so did our first Advent. Unbeknownst to me, I went into that first Advent with much of the ingrained secularized version of the season, thinking of it as Catholic-speak for "Christmas prep" or a countdown in the anticipation of the big day that would come and go on December 25. There were some new additions, however. I started listening to Advent-themed music and signed up for Bishop (then Fr.) Robert Barron's Advent reflections. I also observed other Catholic families during this season, and in their seasonal rhythms I noticed that previously lacking "distinctness" present before my eyes.

Suddenly, about halfway through Advent, a light bulb went on in my head, and joy filled my heart. I saw that Advent was its entirely own season for the Church, one that was of great importance in preparing our hearts to celebrate Christmas. Simultaneously, I realized that, for Catholics, Christmas *begins* on December 25 and it's not over on December 26. Far from it! Every one of the eight days in the "octave" of Christmas emphasizes the joy of Christmas day, and the "The Twelve Days of Christmas" (not just a counting song) take us to Epiphany—the feast that celebrates the wise men meeting Jesus. In America, it is actually "Christmastime" until the Feast of the Baptism of our Lord—about three weeks after Christmas day!

The best part about discovering the Catholic Church's distinctly Christian rhythm for Advent and Christmas was that it is completely *countercultural*. While the rest of society is in a hubbub of shopping and party frenzy the whole month before Christmas, we have been given the quietness of Advent to prepare our hearts for the birth of Jesus. And as secular Christmas rituals are wrapping up, the Church's celebration is just *beginning*. There's no competition with Santa and shopping malls; and the busy running around and stressful pace of packing all the merriment into December is over. I could not believe what a gift I had suddenly been given by the Church, after having received so much already. My heart had been yearning for this kind of difference, this sacred aesthetic and rhythm to the Christmas season for so long; and here was Mother Church, through her ancient liturgical rhythms, focusing our holiday celebration decidedly on Christ.

Moreover, what finally clicked that first Advent was that I was beginning (for the first time) a new liturgical year with the Church. I had entered into the Catholic rhythm of the liturgical calendar, which meant that every day of the next 365 could be just as *distinct* and filled with spiritual purpose as those of my first Advent and Christmas as a new Catholic. My Catholic homecoming took on deeper meaning as I realized the Church's gift in the rhythms of the liturgical year.

Embodied Faith in the Liturgical Year

In observing the liturgical year, beginning afresh every Advent, "the kingdom of God enters into our time,"[66] and we get caught up into the story of salvation history. It is an embodied, sweeping narrative that the Church repeats and relives over and over again. And it's not just for us. We, the visible Church on earth, through participating in the liturgical telling of salvation history, become a vibrant symbol to the whole world of God's pursuit of humanity. The *Catechism* explains that through the rhythm of the liturgical year, Mother Church "unfolds the whole mystery of Christ…. Thus, recalling the mysteries of the redemption, she opens up to the faithful the riches of her Lord's powers and merits, so that these are in some way ***made present in every age***; the faithful lay hold of them and are filled with saving grace."[67]

The liturgical calendar allows every generation—from the first Christians to us today—to celebrate and relive this story in ways unique to each season. Each season works to build an embodied faith in us by focusing us on one particular aspect of salvation history and the life of Christ. We celebrate these seasons and mark their days through various acts of *veneration* and *worship*. We venerate various saints that have gone before us by memorializing their "feast days," displaying their images, asking for their prayers, and retelling their stories—stories that help us along our annual pilgrimage to follow their examples of worship. Our worship of God deepens by spending prolonged periods of time dwelling within the Scriptures and symbol-rich traditions of each season. The symbols contain deep theological meaning for our intellectual conception of God, but they also engage our bodies and our hearts in ***acts*** of worship.

My pre-Catholic approach to Christian holidays was basically intellectual. It involved mostly *thoughts* about the meaning of Christmas or Easter, which means I was *thinking* a lot about Christ; but all of those thoughts did not have embodied connections to worshipping Him in ways particular to that season. Remember, worship is the *practice of desire*. Living the liturgical year is all about worship—participating in an annual cycle of habits that form our desire *for* God. And habits take time to form. The beauty of our Church's liturgical design is that each season brings its own unique faith formation in our lives and hearts; so, over the course of *every* year, our worship of God becomes more complete and more embodied. Let's look at some of the ways each season's embodied habits and liturgical rhythms form our worship of God.

Advent

Waiting. Advent is all about waiting. It is about remembering salvation history's long groaning for a Messiah and slowing down to be in sync with God's timing for our own lives. It is in all ways opposite to the hustle and bustle of the commercial pre-Christmas season. Our churches are bare, unadorned with the festive decorations and trimmings of the holiday to come. In the drab décor we realize our human lack of adornment in our state of sin, the insufficiency of all our human efforts. The songs we sing during mass speak to the waiting of the season and the anticipation of the longed-for Messiah. Catholic singer/songwriter Matt Maher recorded one of my favorite versions of the traditional Advent hymn, "O Come, O Come Emmanuel." Toward the end of the song he builds to a bridge that powerfully speaks of our need to be rescued and our longing for our rescuer, as he sings: "Take heart, oh weary soul, take heart…For help is on its way…And Holy is His name."

Every time I listen to those words my heart is flooded with the full meaning of the Advent season for all of humanity: *Hang on! Help is coming! Dear weary souls who have waited for so long, those burdened and weighed down in this broken world of sin—hang on! Your Redeemer is coming; He's so close; He sees your pain and hears your cries, and He is coming for you.* You see, the truth we realize when we contemplate Advent in the place of our hearts is the truth of the Incarnation—the Word became flesh and dwelt among us (John 1:14). He came to us; and that "coming of our King" is an ever-present phenomenon in our daily lives. But we often forget it, and our hearts get dark with that forgetfulness. We need this Advent season to remind us and bring light to the dark places. The symbol of the Advent wreath in our homes and in our churches paints a beautiful picture of the transformation that's to be going on inside our hearts. Starting Advent, our wreath of four candles is unlit. Then, gradually, it is illuminated as each passing Sunday we light another candle. So too are our hearts—dark and in need of the light of Christ. And as that light gets brighter it illumines our hearts like a torch brought into a dark room. Light moves to every hidden place, revealing the dusty and cobwebbed corners we've neglected. In that revealing light we invite the Holy Spirit to prepare our hearts to receive Christ on Christmas Day.

You can see how we need this time of preparation. We aren't ready on December 1 to start singing, "Joy to the world, the Lord is come..." We only know the full measure of that joy when we have lived a little while without it. The period of Advent is a time to live in that place of longing for our King to come, but we won't long for Him if we have not experienced where we are without Him. Our hearts need to be made ready for hosting our Christ for Christmas, just the way we ready our homes to host the loved ones coming to stay.

Christmas

If Advent is all about waiting for our King, then Christmas is certainly all about welcoming Him! The liturgical Christmas season takes us on a tour of all the "welcomes" Christ received. That welcome celebration begins on Christmas Eve and lasts anywhere from twelve to forty days, depending on the ecclesial tradition you follow. We start on Christmas Day, celebrating the very moment of His birth. He is of course first welcomed in the stable manger by Mary and Joseph, by the animals that He created, and by the humble shepherds from the fields. The excitement around the moment of His birth fills the Octave (first eight days) of Christmas in our churches and in our homes—just like it filled that Bethlehem night sky.

Then on January 6, fulfilling the "twelve days of Christmas," we continue our welcoming celebrations with the Feast of the Epiphany. We celebrate the visit from the magi who followed the star from a great distance, with costly gifts, to bow down and worship this child that must be a king. On the American Catholic calendar the Christmas season ends with the Feast of the Baptism of the Lord, but the Vatican doesn't take down its Christmas decorations until the Feast of the Presentation on February 2, when Mary and Joseph presented Jesus in the temple. Here too, He was welcomed by Simeon and Anna; and this welcome is profoundly important for us to remember as part of our Christmas celebration. Upon seeing Jesus in Mary's arms, Simeon prophesied as one who truly had waited watchfully for his King: "Now, Master, you may let your servant go in peace, according to your word, for my eyes have seen your salvation, which you prepared in sight of all the peoples, a light for revelation to the Gentiles, and glory for your people Israel" (Luke 2:29-32). These words speak a beautiful fulfillment to the longing in Maher's Advent lyrics. And that is just as it should be; for when celebrated in full context together, the Christmas season of welcome is the perfect fulfillment of the Advent season's hopeful longing.

Lent

At the beginning of my first Lent, I remember thinking that forty days was a long time! But I quickly learned that I needed every one of those forty days to get ready for Easter—and I don't mean get my Easter *baskets* ready. I needed the penitential worship of Lent to chip away vice and form virtue so my heart would be ready for the celebratory worship of Easter. I also learned the powerful symbolism of the number forty. We see it throughout Scripture, throughout the story of salvation history. The Israelites wandered in the desert, kept from the Promised Land for forty years. Forty days after Jesus' birth He was presented in the temple. Jesus fasted forty days alone in the desert after His baptism, being tempted there by Satan. And He was with His disciples, appearing to many different people for forty days after His resurrection, which is why the Easter season is forty days too. The increment of forty has great significance within the Catholic calendar year, and in the season of Lent it is forty days spent in a spirit of repentance and reflection on Christ's suffering for our sin.

Before becoming Catholic I celebrated many Easters without celebrating any Lents. But after becoming Catholic I realized that many Catholics probably have as well. We can easily miss the significance if we neglect the gifts the Church offers during this season: the frequent opportunities for confession, the fasts from food on Ash Wednesday and Good Friday, the self-denial of Friday abstinence from meat, praying more communally the Stations of the Cross and the Chaplet of Divine Mercy, and the forty days of personal fasting from our personal "wants" to make room for more of the One we need. At first, we might not describe the embodied faith of Lent as *beautiful*. We might be afraid of the hard work of Lent in our lives; but participating in these challenging Lenten rituals is what makes us ready for Easter. If Christ walked through His Passion, down the road of Calvary to get to Resurrection Sunday, then how can we not walk the Lenten path, dying to self, to get to our Easter morning? In the famous words of Archbishop Fulton Sheen, "Unless there is a Good Friday in your life, there can be no Easter Sunday."

Easter

There is a beautiful mirroring that happens within the cycle of the Church seasons, depicted by the alternating liturgical colors of the vestments and cloths. The color of Advent and Lent is purple; the color of Christmas and Easter is white. Just as Christmas is the perfect fulfillment of Advent, so too is Easter the reward of Lent. Lent may be forty days of denial, of dying to self; but Easter is all about forty days of life, of rejoicing in our resurrected savior of the world. He makes all things new, and His coming to life brings us to life too. Throughout the six weeks of Lent we witness a bare church with icons hidden, to the point that even the crucifix—our ever-present image of Christ—is covered with a purple cloth by the time Holy Week arrives. The resurrection's transforming impact on our souls is depicted symbolically in the Church's visual shifting from Good Friday to Easter morning. The drab, purple-cloaked chapels and altars are transformed with spring lilies and cloths of white. In Christ we are made new creatures. We leave our churches Good Friday night, our sinful nature buried in His death, and we come back Easter Sunday resurrected in His nature, that "we too might live in newness of life."[68]

Ordinary Time

There are two periods during the liturgical year that we call "Ordinary Time." The first follows the Christmas season of welcoming Christ, and the second follows the Easter season of rejoicing in His resurrection. These seasons are filled with various saints' feast days and other special memorial days in salvation history and the life of the Church. Pentecost is one important example. On this day we celebrate Jesus sending His Holy Spirit, the third member of the Godhead, to live within us. By setting aside a specific day to celebrate this event, our theology moves from being merely intellectual knowledge to becoming part of the fabric of our daily lives. By celebrating the lives of saints on given feast days we are acknowledging the truth, beauty, and goodness of lives lived in the light of the resurrection. Their stories compel us to examine the authenticity of our faith, to assess whether we ourselves are living in the light of Christ. As Pope Emeritus Benedict XVI has said, those "who have hope live differently." And in the case of saints who have been martyred, those who have hope *die* differently as well. We celebrate these lives and these deaths so that we *remember*—remember how we are to live, remember our need for a savior, and remember that our home and hope is ultimately found in "the life of the world to come."

The Liturgical Year in Your Life

There is clearly purpose and beauty in living according to the Catholic liturgical calendar. But how do we *do* that? We do that by uniting the rhythms of our daily lives with the rhythms of the liturgical year. The wonderful thing about the diversity of Catholic traditions is that there are many different ways to do this, and no two Catholic homes need to live the liturgical year in the same way. The liturgical seasons provide overarching themes; but you can discern particular practices, traditions, and rituals that fit your cultural background, the personalities within your family, and the aesthetic of your home. By the same token, in reflecting on the seasons of the liturgical year you may discern that rhythms and traditions within your family need to change. Perhaps, like me, your previous approach to Christmas and Easter needs to be refreshed or totally transformed. Let the Holy Spirit show you how your home and the rhythms of your family can better reflect the liturgy of the Church.

While there is much room for diversity in living the liturgical year (and countless resources for doing so in books and online!), there are some guidelines that I have found helpful:

- **Be Intentional** – Regardless of how you celebrate each liturgical season, be *intentional* about it. Think about why your choices are good and what makes them meaningful for you and your family. We all notice intentionality, particularly children. The simplest effort to live the liturgical year, when done with intention, will have significant impact.

- **Make the Season Visible** – Living the liturgical year should not be something that exists only in our minds; we need visual cues to help us cultivate an embodied faith. Find a place to incorporate the season's liturgical color in your home: **purple** for Advent and Lent, **white** for Christmas, Easter, and saints' feast days, and **red** for Pentecost and the feast days of martyrs. Also, use icons and images to denote feast and memorial days. For example, on Saturdays and all of the Blessed Mother's feast days you could put out an image of Mary; and you could do the same with other solemnities, feasts, and memorials as well.

- **Make Sunday Special** – For the Catholic, Sunday should be different. It is our "little Easter" every week. It should stand out for you and your family, and the practices of that day should bring rest to your body and soul. Obviously, we attend mass; but think of other ways to intentionally practice setting this day apart from the rest of the week.

- **Connect Liturgy to Narrative** – The liturgical year tells one sweeping narrative; and it is vital that our practice of following it remains connected to story as well. Start collecting books with the stories of the saints and books with stories themed for each liturgical season. This need not be cost prohibitive; the library is a great resource. While there are many picture books and books on the lives of the saints for children, don't let these be the only books on your shelves. Stories are not just for children! For adults to have a well-formed, embodied faith, we need stories too. We cannot *live out* what we do not *take in*. Have a rich reading life—one that puts you in sync with liturgical rhythms.

- **Celebrate Saint Feast Days** – I am convinced that one cause of Catholics leaving the faith (among many) is that they didn't celebrate the lives of the saints or read their stories growing up. The collective lives of the saints form one of the most powerful apologetics of the Church. These people are our friends and role models, and the example of their lives directs our lives to Christ. When we make their feast days special, when we intentionally ask for their intercession, when we celebrate how they ran their races well and kept the faith, we are infusing life into our own journeys and lifting up our immortal souls.

- **Differentiate between the Church Calendar and the Secular Calendar** – We should be Catholic *first*. Our faith should be the most important thing in our lives. The holidays on the Church calendar should be more important in the rhythm of our lives than secular holidays and rituals; and reflecting on the prominence of the liturgical calendar in our lives can be a good litmus test for how much our faith comes before our ethnicity, nationality, and other cultural backgrounds.

Living the liturgical year should be life-giving to you, because these seasons and feast days are gifts from our Church to build our faith. It should not be a legalistic expression of Catholicism, and it certainly should not feel like drudgery. Rather, these rhythms of the Church should keep you focused on Christ and our home with Him for eternity. Being *at home* in the Church, and living her liturgical year faithfully, is preparation for our eternal rhythms in heaven. In the words of an old spiritual hymn, "This world is not my home; I'm just a passin' through."

Resources for Embodied Faith

The Catholic Catalogue: A Field Guide to the Daily Acts That Make Up a Catholic Life, by Melissa Musick and Anna Keating

This book, written by a mother-daughter duo, is the print counterpart to the popular website TheCatholicCatelogue.com. As the subtitle reflects, this book is really a guide to all things Catholic: the "Smells and Bells" (Part 1), the "Seasons of the Church Year" (Part 2), and the "Seasons of Life" (Part 3). While the entire book will be a fantastic resource for Catholic faith and living, Part 2 offers a helpful guide for syncing daily, weekly, and yearly rhythms of life to the Church's seasons. It also highlights various important activities and feast days within those seasons.

The Catholic Home: Celebrations and Traditions for Holidays, Feast Days, and Every Day, by Meredith Gould

Gould is a Catholic convert whose Jewish background helped her embrace and fully realize the importance of ritual and tradition in the Catholic Church and home. Her book offers an extension of some of the things I've discussed here about embodied faith through living the liturgical year; and she offers specific and meaningful ideas for observing feast days and holidays. She explains why traditions matter in the celebrating and living of our faith throughout the year. In the book's preface she says: "Here you'll find rituals and observances for holy days and feast days on the liturgical calendar that just may transform 'doing' into 'being'." Yes—that's just what we are after.

The Catholic All Year Compendium: Liturgical Living for Real Life, by Kendra Tierney

Kendra has been a popular blogger on liturgical living in the family—among other things—for a while, and this book is jam-packed with plenty of wisdom and ideas for celebrating significant feast days and liturgical seasons throughout the Church year. I really appreciate the combination of how-to-celebrate and why-to-celebrate content throughout the book. This is a liturgical living book to keep handy and reference often.

chapter 5

The Prayers of the Saints: Embodied Faith in Intercession

"Another angel with a golden censer came and stood at the altar; he was given a great quantity of incense to offer with the prayers of all the saints on the golden altar that is before the throne. And the smoke of the incense, with the prayers of the saints, rose before God from the hand of the angel." —Revelation 8:3-4

Discovering the Ultimate "Prayer Warriors"

During our early investigation of Catholic teachings, my interaction with prayer traditions distinct to Catholicism centered on the hot-button topics of prayers to the saints and the rosary. On this point, I should mention two of the main misconceptions of Catholicism that I had been taught in a variety of Protestant denominations: first, that Catholics *worship* the Virgin Mary; secondly, that Catholics pray *to* the saints. Moreover, and probably largely due to these two misconceptions, I had been taught by my high school Sunday school teachers that Catholicism was a *cult*. These claims formed the backdrop of my interaction with Catholicism in general and its prayer practices in particular, and they created a dissonance that had to be resolved. *If this is the true Church of Christ, as a mounting pile of evidence seemed to be demonstrating, then how do I reconcile these seemingly heretical teachings?* No doubt there were many voices of clarity along the way, but I recall Bishop Robert Barron providing one distinctly illuminating narrative in his *Catholicism* series episode on the lives of the saints.[69] His description of the lives of some of the Church's most beloved saints—saints like Katherine Drexel, Therese of Lisieux, Mother Teresa, and Edith Stein—was both enlightening and compelling to a seeker like myself. Up until this point, I had thought of these people as mythical icons with golden halos, religious symbols that seemed to promote something that smacked of idolatry. I suppose what had been formed in my imagination of Catholicism's doctrine of the saints was some sort of Grecian-like structure of demigods and goddesses; and I assumed that Catholics believed these beings to possess divine powers employed for particular favors and petitions. It seemed, from the talk of novenas and other such repetitive prayers, that these "saints" (not unlike the Greek divinities) were fickle and must be petitioned in just the ways that suited their fancies in order for prayers to be granted.

Though this was, more or less, the picture that had been painted for me through strung-together misconceptions, I had my suspicions that I was missing something. Indeed, through listening to Bishop Barron's discourse and then investigating the stories of some of these saints myself, I found that Protestant conceptions of the saints and their role in the Church were entirely askew. As I read about the lives of these men and women, particularly the martyrs, I found myself compelled by their complete abandonment to Christ and detachment from this world at even the highest cost. Far from detracting my worship from God, my absorption into their narratives drew me closer to Christ. I quickly realized the major misconception—Catholics were not petitioning favors from these saints in heaven; they were petitioning the favor of that saint's *intercession to God on their behalf.* It wasn't that the saints would be able to do anything of their own power, but rather by the power of God through their intercession. In the Christian culture of my childhood, the phrase "prayer warrior" was a common label for a Christian who prayed continually and seemed to have a direct line to God. These were the people you went to first if there was a medical emergency or other crisis for which you needed prayer; you knew they would be on their knees petitioning the Father with your requests. In other words, you knew when *they* prayed, God listened and moved. If this was true of men and women that I knew personally, who were still journeying pilgrims with me in this life on earth, how much more would this certainly be the case with the saints in heaven who had finished their races well, achieving perfect abandonment to God's will and forevermore stood in the actual presence of God? Surely, I realized, the saints are the *ultimate* prayer warriors; and I wanted these people to be praying, around the clock, for me.

The more I have studied the lives of the saints, the more I am drawn (in accordance with the Church's directive)[70] to honor or *venerate* them. Why in the world would we do otherwise? Quite frankly, Christians show much more such honor to sports legends and national heroes. And in various Protestant traditions of my childhood we certainly practiced a kind of veneration for missionaries such as Jim Elliott and Amy Carmichael. We didn't call them "saints," but we heralded their lives as exemplars of Christian service and devotion to God. It is a grave loss, one among many of Protestantism's abandoned faith practices, that modern Christian prayer should lack the intercession of these heroes who stand worshiping around the throne of God, their hands *literally* filled with our petitions.[71] Moreover, if we are to honor the saints and follow their examples of Christian living, then it quickly became clear to me that Mary—Christ's own mother and "Queen of the Saints"—was our most important example; her life's example and intercession for us, more than any other person, surely bring us closer to Jesus. When we came into the Church in June 2013, I had embraced a regular practice of invoking the prayers of the saints, especially the Blessed Mother; and I found great solace in praying the mysteries of the rosary. However, I suppose there comes a time, as with all prayer, when you must assess your own faith in the intercession of the saints— whether or not you really believe that they hear and act. The enemy of our souls is the father of many lies, and one of his favorites to whisper is that our prayers fall on deaf ears. My story that follows speaks to the contrary.

It was February 10, 2015, during a particularly bitter-cold winter, and Mike and I sat in the ultrasound exam room while a technician took measurements for baby number three. I was eighteen weeks and five days along in the pregnancy, and this was the exciting moment we were supposed to find out the gender of the baby. The baby wasn't giving us a good look, and as the tech left the room to go get the doctor she said, "I think your dates might be a little off; the baby is only measuring about sixteen weeks old." The doctor came in, and though the anatomy looked good (and he was 90 percent sure it was a girl), he questioned our dating as well, saying that the size discrimination was significant. After chatting about dates, checking my file, and confirming the accuracy of the eight-week ultrasound I had, he realized we were not dealing with a dating discrepancy. We asked what that meant, and he said he couldn't say for sure after only one ultrasound, but the baby should not be measuring two weeks behind. We had to come back in ten days to measure again.

We were a little concerned, and Mike asked what the worst-case scenario would be. The doctor responded that the amniotic fluid level looked a little low, and he was suspicious that the placenta may not be functioning optimally to nourish the baby. But he didn't know how serious of a problem it might be until we gave it more time and measured again. The worst-case would be to come back and see no growth at all. He hoped the baby would just be able to keep up growth. He couldn't really give us more information at that point, but he looked right at me and said this was something *completely out of my control*. If there was a problem with the placenta, it had nothing to do with anything I did or didn't do, and there was nothing that could be done to make a placenta improve in function. I'm sure he didn't realize it, but I sensed the words were prophetic and divinely appointed.

As we prepared to leave the office, Mike and I exchanged concerned glances, knowing it would be a long ten days to wait for more information. I told him I needed to stop in the bathroom and would meet him out front. I went in, locked the door, and stood facing the mirror. I heard the doctor's words in my head—*this is out of your control*. Tears started, and immediately, I thought of the Blessed Mother and her "yes" to the Lord. Mary was pointing out my path to me, and I believed her prayers would cover me while I journeyed on it. I knew what I had to do at that very moment, before I even left the office. In the face of complete uncertainty for what lie ahead, I had to say "yes" to God's will, to the perfect plan He had for my life and the life of the little baby inside of me. "*Yes*, Lord," I said. "Whatever journey is about to start right now, I'm not going to fight Your will; so please give me the grace that I will need."

It was a long ten days. But I could feel the grace and peace as we waited until the next ultrasound on February 20. It was a freezing cold morning at 7 a.m. on the first Friday of Lent—a Lent we will never forget. The room felt chilly as the technician squeezed some gel on my exposed belly and quickly took the measurements she needed for the doctor, who came in a few minutes later to take a look. "Have you been leaking fluid? Bleeding?" he asked. I answered, "No." Then he said I could get cleaned up, and he would meet us in his office to talk. "I'm very concerned," he said, after we were seated. "The baby hasn't grown at all, and there is now less amniotic fluid.

I'm afraid that what I suspected is the case; you have a bad placenta that is just not functioning, and there is nothing we can do to fix that." "What does that mean?" Mike asked. The doctor's response was the worst news I had ever received: "The baby is probably not going to survive more than a couple more weeks. I am going to have to have you come back in one week to see if there is still a heartbeat, since you haven't felt the baby move yet. Once the baby passes, you will have to go to the hospital, and they will induce you so that you can deliver it."

I couldn't get any words out. Mike just asked the questions. I might have said "okay" and reached for the box of tissues he was offering. Our doctor was so kind, expressing his heartfelt sadness for delivering such news. I realized that moments like this must be the worst part of his job. We left the office, but we had driven separate cars, so Mike could go to work. He asked me if I wanted to just leave my car, but I said I would drive myself. On the way home I just cried, "Lord, I'm so sad, and I'm scared." I knew there was no way I would get through the weeks to come on any amount of my own strength; I just prayed for His grace to cover me…one day at a time.

Oh, how we needed prayer. There were questions to face that Mike and I had never dreamed would challenge us. *How do we talk to our almost four-year-old about what is happening? How will I get through laboring and delivering a dead baby? Where would we bury the baby? Will the hospital let us leave with the baby?* Mike spent the weekend calling priests and funeral homes. For every concern that came up, the right person was divinely timed to be there for support. Our parish priests assured us they would take care of everything regarding a burial service, and the baby could be buried in the church's infant graveyard. They recommended funeral homes they had worked with in the past. A dear woman I had gotten to know at church called me as soon as she heard the news on Friday. She put us on the prayer list, and she got me in touch with an amazing local ministry called Isaiah's Promise, which ministers to parents who have had such prenatal diagnoses. I can't explain the peace we had throughout that weekend. We were experiencing the anticipation of an imminent tragedy and the trauma that would come with it; yet, each day had been indelibly marked with divine grace. Mike went to work on Monday, and by this time most of the people he worked with, his students, and our close friends had heard the news. People just kept contacting us to check on us and tell us they were praying. As I was resting during the kids' naptime that afternoon, I felt like I was coming up to the surface for air. I was flipping through my notebook from a Catholic women's group I attended, and I found a pamphlet that was handed out the week before. It was the story of a Catholic woman's miraculous healing. I read about the tumor on her heart valve that inexplicably disappeared as she lay on the operating table ready to be cut open, and tears started running down my face. At that moment, with a small booklet of prayers to St. Gerard (Patron Saint of troubled pregnancies) sitting next to me on my bed, I suddenly felt the grace to pray for my own miracle.

I called Mike and said, "Our little girl is not dead yet. She is still with us, and I am going to ask God for a miracle. I have already given this baby to Him and surrendered to His will for her life. But I can still ask for the miracle, if that is the will of God. I don't know any other way for me to pray right now."

"Honey," he said. "I will definitely pray with you. But it is going to be hard for me to let myself hope for that. I was hoping for that on Friday."

"I know," I said. "But on Friday it wouldn't have been a miracle."

The next day, I started praying a novena to St. Gerard, asking him to intercede with us for a miracle. That night, our associate priest, Fr. Patrick Lewis, came to our home and said a private mass for our family. He gave me a pregnancy blessing, joining with us in our prayer for God to do a miracle. On Wednesday, the same friend who got me in contact with Isaiah's Promise took me to a healing mass at Fr. Dan Leary's parish in Silver Spring, MD. It was beautiful, and after the mass we got in line to be prayed for during Adoration. I knelt on one of the carpet squares near the altar, listening to the musicians and singers, and fixing my gaze on the Blessed Sacrament. When it was my turn, one of the priests came and laid hands on me, and I just basked in the blessing of such special prayer. As I made my way back to the kneeler in my pew, I was overwhelmed with gratitude for the healing Christ was doing in my heart and the grace I was being shown. I looked around that church, and I saw so many extremely sick people—people being helped to the front with Stage IV cancer, children with epilepsy and mental disorders, people with crosses to carry much heavier than mine. Tears just poured down my face as I realized that in the midst of my suffering I had been given every grace I had needed. The words of the Our Father—"Give us this day our daily bread"—had renewed meaning. I had never been as close to Christ as I had in that past week. I was at peace. I left that mass healed—regardless of whether healing occurred inside my womb. I had the love of my Savior; and my life and the life of my little baby had eternal purpose according to His will.

On Friday, one week after the diagnosis, we were back in the ultrasound office to check for a heartbeat. I told Mike I thought I had been feeling the baby move the last couple of days, but I wasn't sure if I was imagining things. The doctor was surprised to find things stable; nothing had gotten worse. The fluid was the same. The heartbeat was good, but they wouldn't be able to measure the baby for another week. We asked what this meant, and our doctor said, "Well, it's not worse." I got the feeling he had been expecting to see either further deterioration or, more likely, a dead baby. He said he would see us in one week, and for the rest of that week we just kept praying. But I started praying for two specific things—increased fluid (which isn't supposed to replenish itself) and growth. I knew everyone, including St. Gerard and the Blessed Mother, joined me in those specific petitions. By this time, we had notified all of our friends, relatives, and the "prayer warriors" at our parish, asking them to pray with us for miraculous healing. People everywhere started praying, and they had their friends, churches, and prayer groups start praying. People who didn't know me from Adam were praying for my baby and me. My friend, Candace, went to every convent website she could think of and listed our baby as a prayer request—basically launching hundreds of Catholic nuns into twenty-four-hour prayer for our baby's life. I had three different groups of women drop off beautifully handmade prayer shawls. Never in my life have I experienced such a tangible, *physical* impact of prayers—I literally *felt* every single one.

Friday morning, March 6, perhaps the coldest morning of the year, Mike and I drove cautiously into Annapolis through snowy, unplowed roads. Schools were closed due to the conditions and the freezing temperatures. My heart tried to hold on to hope with all its might, but I could feel doubt crouching at the door. I remembered a friend's words from the week before: "It's always darkest right before the dawn." Yes, it might be a cliché; but some people find prayers and faith cliché too when they haven't experienced the substance of their truth and power. All of a sudden, we came over a hill on the highway, and in the sky that had been gray and hazy a beautiful sunrise was breaking through the clouds. Inside my heart I heard the voice of hope that had been sustained through all the prayers of the saints—those of earth and heaven—*hang on!*

The technician took us back and got started taking measurements. I tried not to pepper her with questions, because I knew she wouldn't tell me anything definitive. But after a couple of minutes I did ask, "There's a heartbeat, right?" "Oh, yes," she responded quickly. "I always check for that first." She finished up as quickly as she could, and said the doctor would be right in. When our doctor walked in, he asked if I had experienced any new symptoms or felt the baby move that week. I said I thought I had felt movement, as he took a second look at things on the monitor. "The crazy thing is," he said after a few seconds, "there is *more* amniotic fluid than last week…" My heart skipped a beat, and suddenly I knew what he was about to say next: "…and the baby has almost doubled in size!" I had hoped so many times over the past two weeks to hear those very words, and here he was speaking them. It was the craziest out-of-body experience. I was speechless, stunned—it was a miracle, and it was happening inside my own body! I just smiled and look at Mike as tears started flowing. Mike pressed him with questions, and then he saw something on the screen that made him ask, "Are you still sure it's a girl?" "Well, no we're not," he responded. "It's hard for me to make out completely with the baby's position, but it looks like it's a boy." Our third boy, indeed, it was.

My doctor was very clear as he sat in his office with us—he had no medical explanation for the results we were seeing. There was clearly something wrong with my placenta from the pictures of it; it had even been bleeding a little into the amniotic fluid. "However," he said, "that can't be the whole problem; if it was, then things wouldn't get better. Fluid doesn't replenish itself like this. I have no explanation for you. Sometimes in medicine we get surprised."

"I don't need an explanation," I said. "We have had a lot of people praying for us and this baby."

"Well," he said, "can whoever has been praying for you pray for me too?"

From that point on, and it was a pregnancy filled with many other moments of divine intervention, my doctor called him the "miracle baby." But we now had to come up with a boy's name. While I was hospitalized with a very bad urinary tract infection, which stressed the baby's heartbeat and nearly caused an emergency C-section around the week he had just reached "viability,"

Hannah's words in 1 Samuel 1:20 came to mind: "She conceived and, at the end of her pregnancy, bore a son whom she named Samuel. 'Because I asked the Lord for him.'" Our little Samuel Gerard, against all predictions, made it all the way to the end of my pregnancy. He was induced at thirty-eight weeks, and quickly made up for his five-pound, nine-ounce birth weight; in a short few months he had joined his brother's growth patterns in the ninetieth percentile for height and weight. Sam's story is a complete testimony to the power of the prayers of Christians on earth joined with the saints in heaven.

Embodied Faith and the Prayers of the Saints

We frequently hear folksy talk of "Grandma looking down on us from heaven," and people smile sweetly at such sentiments. Yet, in reality, we live as if there exists a great barrier between us and them, between us walking around down here on earth and those we believe have made it to the other side. Perhaps there is no area in which modernism has desensitized us to the supernatural more than in regard to our access to divine grace through the saints' intercession. The enemy of our souls knows that his lies are most effective when we don't see reality clearly, and the heavy curtain of modernity's distractions keep us from perceiving the realm of the supernatural. The last thing Satan wants when he is waging war on your soul—and make no mistake, there is a *battle* going on for your soul[72]—is for you to enlist these prayer warriors alongside you in battle. But we can take courage that we are on the winning side and we have only to ask the angels and saints to fight with us. Our Church, our home of refuge during the battles of this life, directs us to petition the saints for intercession:

> The witnesses who have preceded us into the kingdom, especially those whom the Church recognizes as saints, share in the living tradition of prayer by the example of their lives, the transmission of their writings, and their prayer today. They contemplate God, praise him and constantly care for those whom they have left on earth. When they entered into the joy of their Master, they were "put in charge of many things." We can and should ask them to intercede for us and for the whole world.[73]

And they *want* to intercede for us! St. Therese of Lisieux famously said, "I will spend my heaven doing good upon earth." Our Blessed Mother, with her mother's heart, longs for us to rest under the mantle of her intercession. Every apparition of Mary involves her request for us to join with her in prayer. She asks us to pray the rosary because its mysteries lead us to Christ; as we meditate on each mystery we are drawn into submission to the will of the Father because we are following the footsteps of Christ and His mother. Mary's *yes*, her *Fiat*—"Be it done unto me according to thy word"—is the model for our prayer and our living.[74]

Throughout the centuries, our Church has offered us many tactile and tangible means of connecting with the saints and experiencing their intercession. But do we Catholics in the twenty-first century first world *really* believe what we profess in our creeds: "…the communion of saints…the resurrection of the body, and the life everlasting"[75]? To be sure, there is a reason we are to *speak* these words at Mass every Sunday. The embodied design is that truth proclaimed through our mouths would make its way from our heads to our hearts. Yet we are regularly indoctrinated with alternate embodied messages and practices, ones of disenchantment. The skepticism and problematic rationalism of the modern age has diminished the mystical, making it exceedingly difficult to live like we believe in a supernatural world at all, and certainly difficult to interact with the spirits that inhabit it. Nonetheless, the Church offers us many embodied means of accessing the supernatural realm and living as if heaven is indeed the greatest reality and our ultimate destination. The relics left behind by martyrs, the documented stories of uncorrupted bodies of saints throughout history, the "living" writings of saints incorporated into the prayers of the Church, the apparitions, the miraculous healings—

all these signs tear down modernity's heavy curtain, reminding and reassuring us that the supernatural is real and the heavenly beatific vision in which these holy men and women rest awaits us too.

Friendship with the Saints

As I have grown into a more embodied faith, I have realized that prayer is relational—not just a personal relationship between me and God, but that it encompasses all of the body of Christ, those here on earth and those blessed in heaven. If our life of prayer, as the *Catechism* tells us, is the substance of our relationship with God—the means by which we sustain it[76]—then is not much of our faith sustained by our communion with fellow believers…those present and those who have gone before us who join with us in our prayers? As my husband and I were going through our condensed and personalized version of the Rite of Christian Initiation for Adults (RCIA) class, the priest mentioned we needed to pick confirmation saints pretty soon, as the date for us entering the Church was fast approaching. Well, that seemed (to a thorough researcher like me) to be an overwhelming task. How could I narrow it down? I would need more time to select the *perfect* saint for me. In retrospect, it was such a silly, and rather self-absorbed, thought. Our priest rattled off a few saints he thought would be wonderful choices, and he mentioned St. Catherine of Siena more than once.

After deliberating for a couple of weeks, and checking out Catherine's saintly stats, I thought I couldn't go wrong with her. But I didn't really have a personal reason for picking her.

It wasn't until a couple of years later, when I was reading Sigrid Undset's masterful biography of St. Catherine, that I was moved to tears; I suddenly realized why I was led to choose her…perhaps why she chose me. Though a saint with profound mystical experiences, Catherine had a very public role in the life of the Church to persuade Pope Gregory XI to leave France—where popes had been living for sixty-seven years—and come back to Rome where he belonged. She corresponded with the pope and many other people through letters dictated to secretaries, as she herself was illiterate. Her role in the corporate Church life was often public and prophetic, though she would have been happy to remain in cloistered prayer all of her days. As a writer, I found in her a holy friend who knew what it was like to have prophetic messages placed on her heart, words that God meant her to speak in public environments for the edification of the whole Church. I might not be carrying on personal correspondence with a pope, but Catherine's empathetic prayers would sustain my faithfulness in writing whatever and to whomever God wanted. From that point on, I had a much closer friendship with St. Catherine than I had before.

We become friends with the saints, with the Blessed Mother, simply by accepting their invitation and desire for friendship. We let them journey with us, and we accept the gift of heavenly friends and invite them to do good for us on earth. I believe we should interact with them in two significant ways: first, by learning from the example of their lives; and second, by inviting them to pray with us.

We learn from their examples by *living* as they did in their stories. All saints' stories remind us that they were people just like us, with temptations and trials just like you and me. But they saw the eternal quite clearly, they developed hearts ripe for daily conversion, and they were able to get to the point of total surrender to God's will. Once we are intimately acquainted with the lives of the saints, then we can begin to live like them; and when we begin to live like them, they lead us to heaven. It's just a hunch, but I would be willing to bet that most people that walk away from the Church didn't ever get to know and develop real *friendships* with the lives of Her saints. Who you are friends with matters; whose example you fashion your own lifestyle after matters as well. Heavenly friendships will lead us to heaven; so, one of the most important embodied faith practices involves immersing ourselves in the stories of the saints.

When we enter into this deeper friendship with the saints, we cannot help but be drawn to them in prayer and ask for them to intercede for us. Asking for prayer is ultimately an act of humility; we are recognizing our need of divine grace and we are willingly revealing that need to others who have a hand in obtaining it for us. But experiencing the fruit of prayer in our lives involves practice, and that means regularly praying the rosary and novenas. When we pray the rosary, we draw close to our holy mother. As our lips repeat each "Hail Mary" our hearts are moved to imitate her submission to God's will. As we meditate on each mystery of the rosary we are imagining our own lives being shaped according to Christ's example of holiness. Novenas are powerful tools of prayer too. They help us enter into a deeper communion with the saints, particularly saints with whom we share common ailments or experiences. Perhaps most importantly, they help unite our wills with the will of the Father. Saints are ultimately the perfect prayer warriors for us because they have said, "not my will, but thine be done."

Resources for Embodied Faith
Lives of the Saints: For Everyday of the Year, by Alban Butler

Butler's original *Lives of the Saints* is a cherished Catholic classic. This book takes his stories and arranges them according to the saints' memorial days, giving readers one or two saint stories for every day of the year. Following the stories are short "lessons" to be learned from each saint's life.

Saint of the Day: The Definitive Guide to the Saints, by Leonard Foley, O.F.M. and Patrick McCloskey, O.F.M

Some people describe this book as a modern version of Butler's *Lives of the Saints*. It is organized similarly to the resource listed above, with one or two saints for every day of the year. Each entry includes a short narrative of the saint's life, a concise "comment" for reflection, and a quote from that saint.

Saints for Young Readers for Every Day (two volumes), by Susan Helen Wallace and Jamie H. Aven

Though this set is out of print, there are copies to be had fairly easily. As with the two resources above, there is one saint's story for every day of the year. (Since it was published in 1995, new saints will be missing.) After each short story, there is a one- or two-sentence reflection on how children (or adults) could ask for that saint's intercession. We personally use this book for our family devotional time each morning. It works quite well for reading aloud to children of all ages, or as independent reading for fluent readers. The stories are beautifully written, and they handle harsh realities of some saint's lives in appropriate ways for innocent ears.

chapter 6

Union with God: Embodied Faith in Private Prayer

"The need to involve the senses in interior prayer corresponds to a requirement of our human nature. We are body and spirit, and we experience the need to translate our feelings externally. We must pray with our whole being to give all power possible to our supplication."
—*The Catechism of the Catholic Church*[77]

Discovering Catholic Prayer

O ne of the most significant epiphanies of becoming Catholic was discovering that my conception of "prayer" was indeed quite small.

I had been a praying Christian all of my life, to be sure. But most of my prayers were spontaneous petitions or expressions of thanks for specific gifts God had provided. I think I was always ready to give God credit for all good things that came into my life, and I certainly had faith that God answered prayer; I had witnessed as much in plenty of circumstances. I was also eager to go to God in prayer, as I quite naturally regarded Him as benevolent and the author of all that was good. Dorothy Day spoke of the fact that it was her happiness in life that drew her to prayer, rather than the presence of despondence or her need of something from Him.[78] My own experience resonates with hers. The perceived goodness of God and joy in life (rather than painful circumstances) led me to prayer also, for I intuitively believed He *wanted* to talk to me, that He desired to *commune* with me.

Though I had the desire, I had not received much specific guidance to facilitate a deep life of prayer, at least not beyond what seemed obvious from Scripture. I realized the power in calling on the name of "Jesus" (Acts 3:6,16), and I knew I was to "pray without ceasing" (1 Thess. 5:17). Church pastors and teachers generally directed me to have my "quiet time" every day, when I read my Bible and talked to God. Such advice is more than many kids are blessed with, and throughout my adolescence I made the effort to reserve time for God. I have no doubt God graciously met my novice efforts with the gift of His presence. But there was much I did not know about how one grows closer to God in prayer and sustains a life of prayer, particularly in challenging circumstances. My prayer life lacked the direction and nourishment of thousands of years of Church teaching and the wisdom of spiritual masters who had themselves experienced regular mystical union with God. But I would not realize this deficit in personal prayer until a few years after becoming Catholic, and it wasn't until more recent history that I would discover the practice of mental prayer.

Looking back, I would say my prayer life had two deficiencies, but both are intrinsically linked together. First, I lacked a solid understanding, both biblical and historical, of Christian mysticism. Other than the miraculous accounts of the apostles in the New Testament, I was completely unfamiliar with the lives of Catholic saints throughout the ages who experienced regular mystical union with God. I grew up familiar with the modern-day charismatic movement to some degree (though my family was in and out of that scene), but I had no depth of perspective in terms of the progression of the mystical practices of believers from the beginning of the Church to present times. As I've said before, I basically missed out on 1,500 years of Church history; and wrapped up in those missing centuries are the stories of countless Christians who experienced supernatural union with God in their daily lives of prayer. I'm certainly not alone in this regard. Modern Christians and Catholics live in a world that is totally skeptical of supernatural experiences. Modern sensibilities have created a limited "realm of possibilities" for the faith life and prayer practices of the twenty-first-century Christian. Skepticism of the supernatural has so permeated society that few within the Church have a *desire* for mystical encounters with God, much less the expectation that they are possible or could even be regular occurrences.

The second deficiency of my prayer life was a misunderstanding of the role our emotions play in the life of prayer. I grew up in a faith tradition that placed high value on emotional experiences—the emotional response to an "altar call," the emotional pacing and climax of praise and worship services, the state of a person's emotions in entering a time of prayer, etc. In fact, heightened emotions seemed to be the litmus test for determining the *authenticity* of a faith experience. Therefore, I came to believe that deep faith experiences in worship and prayer would (and should) be accompanied by intense emotional stimuli. And this was and is a common occurrence for the young person raised in the Evangelical tradition.

I believe there is a correlation between this emotionalism and a lacking mysticism. It is as if Catholics and Christians throughout the ages have gradually acquiesced to modern sensibilities, abandoning expectations of mystical experiences more and more, and filling the void left with a pursuit of emotional experiences. Emotions and feelings are, after all, highly valued cues in determining reality for the self in modern culture; there are many sources of input influencing us to rely on our emotions in deciphering reality. There are frequent appeals to "feel-good" spirituality at every turn. But here's the problem with a disenchanted view of reality that doesn't allow for mystical encounters with God, while simultaneously conjuring up emotional responses—*at some point we won't feel like praying.* Perhaps at many points we will not get the warm fuzzies at the thought of time with God, nor will we be naturally inclined to pray. *What do we do then?* Indeed, that is the question I had ultimately encountered in seeking a deeper life of prayer as a new Catholic. As I investigated the Catholic prayer tradition, I found a great arsenal of tools at my disposal. These spiritual disciplines of prayer were centuries old, had produced many saints, and (no surprise) most definitely involved *embodied* faith practices.

Embodied Faith in Prayer

A prayer life is not an optional element in a Catholic's faith. Prayer is *vital*. Without it, we lack a personal relationship with God. Our faith is *proclaimed* by our belief (the creed), *celebrated* corporately as the body of

Christ (the sacramental liturgy), and *lived out* faithfully through prayer, which is the substance of our "personal relationship" with God.[79] The embodied practice of prayer is our sustenance and the means by which we *live out* our faith and are drawn into a closer union, with God. To be in *relationship* with someone means you *talk with* that person. The God of Christianity is not a dualistic god disengaged from us or disinterested in how we live our lives. Neither does He want us to merely *acknowledge* Him. What deep relationships do we know that simply involve one's thoughts about the other person? Those whom we love, we love not with the mind alone, but ultimately with the *heart*. Our triune God has invited us into a relationship with Him—Father, Son, and Holy Spirit. He is deeply in love with us and desires to dwell within us.[80] Therefore, the goal of any prayer practice is to love God with our hearts, to unite our hearts with the heart of Christ.

Catholic prayer rituals and practices engage our bodies, voices, and minds together in a progression of prayer that moves us into deeper union with God. All prayer—whether vocal or mental—originates from the heart, as we read over a thousand times in Scripture,[81] and it is *through* our bodies (rather than being disconnected from them) that we develop a heart-to-heart union with God. The Church divides prayer into three types: **vocal prayer**, **meditation**, and **contemplative prayer**. The interwoven thread connecting the three is "the recollection of the heart."[82] In other words, all prayer practices of the Church transform us into better *lovers* of God. By engaging in rhythms of Catholic prayer—vocal, meditative, and contemplative—the believer is renewed and sustained through an embodied, and grace-filled, progression of prayer: our hearts are primed to move toward love (vocal prayer); the state of our hearts is considered and confronted (meditation); and our hearts are ignited with the fire of mystical love (contemplative prayer). In examining these three types of prayer, we see the dynamic role each one plays in forming our desire for God and fitting us for our heavenly home.

Vocal Prayer

We enter into prayer at all times as whole persons, an important truth which the Church rightly affirms and directs us to embrace. "Vocal prayer, founded on the union of body and soul in human nature, associates the body with the interior prayer of the heart, following Christ's example of praying to His Father and teaching the Our Father to His disciples."[83] The glorious mystery of the Incarnation, of God becoming man, allowed Christ (with His own body) to model prayer for us in our bodies. The Church's tradition of vocal prayer is rich and deep, providing us with more beautiful prayers than we could pray in a lifetime. There are the prayers we pray often: the Sign of the Cross, the Our Father, the Hail Mary, the

Glory Be, the Rosary, the Angelus, the Blessing Before Meals, etc. We also have the prayers of the Mass (i.e., Gloria, Sanctus, etc.) and the prayers of all liturgies and rites. In addition, we are blessed with four volumes of prayers in *The Liturgy of the Hours* to pray at several periods throughout each day. Beyond all of these, the personal prayers of saints throughout the ages have been handed down to us, providing immense inspiration for our personal devotion and prayer lives.

While we have unlimited *resources* for vocal prayer, what is more important is that the Church has provided us with *formational rhythms*—daily, weekly, and seasonally—for engaging in these prayers. A Catholic's day may include the rituals of a Morning Offering, Morning Prayer, daily Mass, the Rosary, and various aspirations (short prayers like, "Jesus, I trust in You!") at any given moment. Sunday Mass, prayers offered in Confession or Adoration, and the Chaplet of Divine Mercy prayed on a Friday afternoon are just some of the prayer practices that create weekly rhythms of grace in our lives. Prayers offered during certain seasons or feasts in the liturgical year—such as Stations of the Cross during the Fridays of Lent—help orient our lives to the life of Christ throughout the year. In this way, as we regularly and purposefully align our lives with the prayers of the Church—body, mind, and soul—our hearts are opening up to the will of the Father, just as Jesus led us to pray.

Meditation

The habits of regular vocal prayer prepare our bodies and hearts to enter into a deeper level of prayer with God—mental prayer. Fr. Jacques Philippe says mental prayer is "prayer that consists of facing God in solitude and silence for a time in order to enter into intimate, loving communion with him." Meditation and contemplative prayer are both forms of mental prayer, happening interiorly in silence. Let's look at meditation first. The Church describes meditation as a "quest" that "engages thought, imagination, emotion, and desire." In pondering insights from spiritual books and Scripture, we are able to let truth confront our own personal lives and reality. "To the extent that we are humble and faithful, we discover in meditation the movements that stir the heart and we are able to discern them."[84] This is the kind of prayer that assesses the condition of our hearts, helps us know the roots of sin in our lives, and opens our hearts up to the truth. But our sense of reality will never be confronted without humility and honesty. Scripture reminds us, "The heart is devious above all else; it is perverse—who can understand it?"[85] Our hearts are capricious things. We think we know them and are their masters; we have justifications for all that we hold onto within them. But Scripture tells us that only God knows the true state of our hearts, and it is He who must reveal to us our heart's condition. As we meditate in silence for a time with the lights of spiritual truth and Scripture, God begins to illuminate the ways our hearts are diseased with sin. But we have to be willing to look honestly at what is there. As C. S. Lewis observes, we should "lay before Him what is in us, not what ought to be in us."[86]

It is then that transformation takes place. In stilling our bodies and quieting our minds, which are both extremely susceptible to the world's distractions around them, we are able to hear the still, small voice of the Holy Spirit speaking within our hearts. The great exchange is offered to us. He wants us to give Him our hearts of stone, and He will give us hearts of *flesh*, fashioned after the heart of Christ.[87] St. Charles Borromeo said, "…in meditation we find the strength to bring Christ to birth in ourselves and in other men."[88] When our hearts change, so does everything else in our beings.[89] This is the embodied work of prayer in the Catholic tradition; we become transformed into the image of Christ. Lectio divina (an ancient form of praying with Scripture), Ignatian methods of meditation, and pondering the mysteries of the rosary are all examples of meditative prayer that help each of us to hear the Lord speaking, revealing the condition of our hearts. Meditation "is of great value, but," as the Church reminds us, "Christian prayer should go further: to the knowledge of the love of the Lord Jesus, to union with him."[90]

Contemplative Prayer

We see the progression that is taking place here. We are moving into a deeper life of prayer. Our hearts are primed to hear the voice of God. Then they are confronted with the image of Christ and transformed into His likeness. When transformation takes place, when we take the new heart He is offering us, we are being prepared to enter into union with God. This is contemplative prayer, where we enter into "silent love"[91] with our Lord; and this is where we reclaim the mystical in our lives. Simply put: "Contemplation is a gaze of faith, fixed on Jesus."[92] Contemplative prayer is nothing short of practicing what we are meant to spend eternity experiencing in our heavenly home. Catholicism's rituals, liturgies, and symbols give our minds and hearts fertile images of what is taking place in deep, personal prayer with God. I love the way the *Catechism* compares our entry into contemplative prayer to the Eucharistic sacrifice of the Mass:

> … we "gather up" the heart, recollect our whole being under the prompting of the Holy Spirit, abide in the dwelling place of the Lord which we are, awaken our faith in order to enter into the presence of him who awaits us. We let our masks fall and turn our heart back to the Lord who loves us, so as to hand

ourselves over to him as an offering to be purified and transformed.[93]

In our liturgies, we are walking out with our bodies and displaying before the eyes of our mind the way that we are to bring our hearts to God. The great saints of the Church did not miss this connection, and their deeply mystical experiences in personal prayer were most certainly fed by their devotion to the Eucharist and their frequent participation in the sacrifice of the Mass. For it is the Eucharist that "contains and expresses all forms of prayer," being "the pure offering" and "*the* sacrifice of praise."[94] St. Therese said, "For me, prayer is a surge of the heart; it is a simple look turned toward heaven, it is a cry of recognition and of love, embracing both trial and joy."[95] More than any other practice, contemplative prayer sustains us in this life and makes us saints.

Praying with the Church

I like to think of the cooperation of vocal and mental prayer as a journey of the heart in relationship with God. Being that the body provides the dwelling place for the soul, the vocal prayers that engage our senses and physically turn our bodies to postures of prayer also help to transition our souls into spiritual attitudes of prayer. The vocal prayers of the Church direct our minds and bodies to Christ, and they start our hearts on the path toward *union* with Him. What is happening here with the prayer tradition of the Catholic Church is the same thing that is happening at other times with her various symbols and rituals—Mother Church is directing us homeward. When we get where we are going, we will continuously behold the beatific vision. We will experience perfect union with God. During this life we are to practice gazing on our Lord, and we will experience heavenly moments of union with Him. As with any spiritual practice, a deeper life of prayer requires direction. We need to be open to the guidance of the Church as we form our prayer habits, as she provides great wisdom on *when* and *how* to pray using vocal prayers, meditation, or contemplative prayer.

In regard to the *when*, Scripture directs us to "pray at all times in the Spirit";[96] however, "we cannot pray 'at all times' if we do not pray at specific times, consciously willing it."[97] If we think prayer will simply *happen* on its own at some point throughout the day, then we are not being honest about our natural inclination to put it off for any number of other pressing matters at hand. We may, in eschewing rigidity, say we do not need to follow a "schedule" of prayer. However, failing to schedule prayer usually results in its lack of primacy in our daily routines. Though there are many ways we may set aside time for personal prayer throughout the day, the Church helps us to set aside specific times for prayer, for she is universally praying at particular times of the day; and there is great benefit in entering into some of these set occasions of prayer. The prayers of The Liturgy of the Hours, or The Divine Office, occur at seven periods[98] throughout the day: Morning Prayer (Lauds), Midmorning Prayer (Terce), Midday Prayer (Sext), Midafternoon Prayer (None), Evening Prayer (Vespers), Night Prayer (Compline), and the Office of Readings, which may be prayed at any point within the day. Of these seven, the most important hours of prayer (the ones of first choice for laypeople) are Lauds, Vespers, and the Office of Readings. The Second Vatican Council emphasized the embodied nature and spiritual enrichment in praying with other Catholics around the world at these times and with these specific prayers: "The divine office, because it is the public prayer of the Church, is a source of piety, and nourishment for personal prayer. And therefore priests and all others who take part in the divine office are earnestly exhorted in the Lord to attune their minds to their voices when praying it."[99]

Praying these prayers of the Church, which include vast amounts of Scripture, will naturally align our wills with the will of the Father and direct our hearts to desire Him above all else. Moreover, they are the best kinds of vocal prayers to help prime our hearts for the deeper levels of mental prayer and union with God. In scheduling prayer throughout our day, it is important to prioritize meditation and contemplative prayer. These types of prayer will certainly not occur without intention, since they require more effort and particular preparations. The Church wisely counsels us to be intentional and persistent in pursuing prayers of "silent love" with God: "One does not undertake contemplative prayer only when one has the time: one makes time for the Lord, with the firm determination not to give up, no matter what trials and dryness one may encounter."[100] And make no mistake; you will experience dryness and difficulty in your quiet prayer time with the Lord. Remember the question I posed earlier—*What do we do when we don't feel like praying?* Thankfully, the Church has plenty of advice when it comes to the *how*, especially during times of difficulty.

As with the other chapters, I have included some resources at the end of this one. These are some of the most helpful books I have personally read on how to pray, specifically how to approach meditation and contemplative prayer. These authors have helped to concisely assemble significant amounts of wisdom from saints throughout the centuries, saints who experienced profound and mystical lives of prayer. You have to get into these books yourself, and they are easy reads. However, I want to preview for you the kinds of practical spiritual advice you will encounter:

- Preparation for prayer
- Methods for entering into and progressing in prayer
- How to deal with dryness in prayer
- How to handle distractions during prayer
- When to set aside time for mental prayer
- How long to devote to contemplative prayer
- The spiritual reading or Scripture best suited to mental prayer

Practicing meditation and contemplative prayer requires effort; even the commitment to regular vocal prayer does not happen easily. If it did, more people would pray this way. But this is the gateway to deeper union with God, and this is the activity of the heart that will prepare us for heaven. Praying with the Church and according to her guidance will truly lead us home to the heart of Christ. And on our journey, a reverse embodiment will take place; as our interior lives are transformed, our exterior lives will be made new as well. "For it is out of the abundance of the heart that the mouth speaks."[101] What is inside of us—that renewed heart of flesh that comes from intimate union with our Lord—will flow out of us and transform our lives, our families, and our world. Christ is calling us to a deeper life of prayer that will transform us into saints—saints whose stories will leave an indelible mark on the world when we finally join the others around the throne.

Resources for Embodied Faith
Time for God, by Fr. Jacques Philippe

This book gets right to the heart of what contemplative prayer and union with God are. It's an accessible examination of the life of prayer for the person living in modern times, as it shares age-old truths from spiritual masters with contemporary examples and application. This is a must-read on the life of prayer.

Meditation and Contemplation: An Ignatian Guide to Praying with Scripture, by Fr. Timothy Gallagher

And this is a second must-read on prayer. For most people, meditation and contemplative prayer are daunting spiritual practices; but that is just because we don't do a good job of discipling people in these practices within the Church today. Fr. Gallagher, like Fr. Philippe, has written many practical books on important spiritual practices of the Church, and this one is no exception. It provides a step-by-step guide and vital wisdom for beginning these prayer practices in our lives.

The Liturgy of the Hours

This is the four-volume set of books we use to pray The Divine Office of the Church throughout the day. For beginners, I would recommend ordering the "St. Joseph Guide for the Liturgy of the Hours." It is a small, inexpensive pamphlet that is published each year; and it provides the exact pages for the various prayers each day.

Praying The Divine Office is a wonderful way to anchor our prayer lives in the rhythms of the liturgical year, as well as to practice praying the words of Scripture, especially the Psalms.

chapter 7

The Cross: Embodied Faith in Redemptive Suffering

"In the cross of Christ not only is the Redemption accomplished through suffering, but also human suffering itself has been redeemed."
—St. Pope John Paul II[102]

Discovering Redemption in Suffering

I have always been a rules follower and a "good girl" by nature. I was the kid that felt great affirmation at the praise of parents or the acknowledgement of work well done by others, and I enjoyed being pleasing to people. My experiences in life seemed to reinforce the idea that things went well for those who followed best practices and diligently completed each step required to get to an ultimate goal. I was also quite reasonable and measured, not fearful, but always careful to avoid undue risks. It is almost impossible for a person like that not to develop the skewed mindset, however consciously or unconsciously, that good preparation and adherence to rules insure a life free of much pain. This perspective gets reinforced in adolescence and the early years of young adulthood, when you grow up with very little suffering and live a relatively charmed, first-world life. The mindset may be perpetuated still further when the Bible is presented (well meaningly, albeit falsely) as "God's simple handbook of rules for the good life." Yes, it's true; our foolish behavior and stubborn pride get us into plenty of needless pain and trouble in life. But that doesn't mean our performance or our goodness is able to create a "safe room" that preserves us from suffering.

In terms of being aware of suffering and tragedy in the world, I was not a terribly sheltered child. My parents had been involved in prison ministry when I was little, and I lost three of my four grandparents somewhere between the ages of six and sixteen. I had been on mission trips to impoverished countries during junior high and high school. When I was thirteen, my mom, sister, and I went with a medical mission team to two Ukrainian orphanages. We played with children who were missing limbs and needed teeth extracted, whose parents had either died or abandoned them on the doorstep, often in desperate response to the 80 percent unemployment in the city at that time. I knew people who died from cancer and other terrible illnesses, even very young children. I knew that suffering, pain, and death were the result of the Fall, of humanity living in a broken world. But the broken world feels "out there" when really painful things have only happened to others and not us. Prior to my thirties, I myself had experienced comparatively little suffering. That changed in the summer of 2013.

The summer our family came into the Church was the same summer my mom was diagnosed with Alzheimer's disease. We had been noticing some memory issues and other odd behaviors in her here and there for a couple of years, but we had been unsuccessful in getting her to see a doctor. Finally, we persuaded her to visit a neurologist at Johns Hopkins in Baltimore. My dad, my sister, and I (with my three-month-old in hand) sat in a small, sterile office separate from Mom, listening to the doctor deliver his diagnosis. We were stunned. Though both my grandmothers had Alzheimer's, one much more severely than the other, this wasn't even on our radar. Mom was in her mid-sixties and had followed a very strict diet as a health writer and researcher for a couple of decades. This was the last news we ever expected to get, and it was a crushing blow to everyone in the family. As would be expected, we all experienced our own unique responses to the diagnosis and to Mom's gradual decline over the months and years that followed. There was, of course, a whole host of varying emotions: denial, anger, sadness, shock, frustration, fear, and many others, as we all felt our way through the nightmare of having a parent and spouse slowly forget her life and, to varying degrees, us.

As Mom's condition grew worse, we realized she shouldn't be alone while Dad worked, but she was not at all comfortable with a stranger helping her at the house. So, over the next few years Mom gradually spent more and more time at my house with me and the kids. She loved being around us, and she would fold all my clothes and stack building blocks with the kids (or by herself). I count it a privilege that I got to spend those months and years with her, in the daily rhythm of quotidian tasks. I was blessed by her cheerful attitude and growing childlike outlook that constantly challenged me to stop and recognize the beauty and gift of the moment. But this period of life also involved a lot of suffering.

There were the obvious sufferings: watching the mother you love be ravaged by a horrible disease, accepting the changing nature of our mother-daughter roles, helping my children process the changes in Nana, or feeling powerless as a brilliant and expressive woman loses her ability to read words and follow a conversation. But there were other sufferings of the heart that were much more private and unexpected; my internal pain and loss revealed surprising heart issues in myself. Though I loved my mom dearly and was always quite close to her, during her illness and decline I found myself experiencing frustration, anger, and resentment. I tried to rationalize my feelings and argue with myself: *You can't be frustrated with her behavior; how unfair is that?* I knew she had no control over what was happening to her, but there was a disconnect between my reasoning and my reaction. And God revealed some deep truth to me as I took the time to examine my conscience and search my heart. I had buried feelings of anger and resentment that were now surfacing, and my issues of control and pride were making themselves known as well. My mom and I had a good relationship; but, like a lot of mothers and daughters, we had our conflicts too. I found that not only was I grieving the gradual and impending loss of my mother, but I was also mourning my lack of control over the past. There were conversations I would have liked to have had, things she and I needed to talk out and work through; but we would never be able to do that now. I wanted closure in certain aspects of our relationship, and the realization that I wasn't going to have it was triggering my anger and resentment.

I think we tend to think of suffering as this unjust thing that brings pointless pain. And much of the time suffering is undeserved; and that makes it tough to accept, but it doesn't make it pointless. What God started showing me in the suffering of my mom's illness was that suffering could be redemptive, and it could transform brokenness into blessedness. Suffering revealed my hidden anger that was blocking love, and it led me to honesty about my own sin and lack of forgiveness of past hurts. I saw redemption in my parents' relationship as well. My mom and dad, like a lot of married couples, certainly had their fair share of arguments and angry words with each other over the years; but the patience and tenderness with which Dad has cared for Mom during her life-altering illness have given all new meaning to the vows "for better or for worse." His love in action toward her, his agency for her quality of life, his preservation of her dignity—all at tremendous cost to himself—have been transforming vehicles of grace in both their lives. In witnessing his self-sacrificing love of her, I can say with certainty that any brokenness from their past has been redeemed. Such love amidst suffering has the power to transform even our greatest faults and turn us into saints. And herein lies a key to interacting with suffering in our lives—we won't experience redemption in our earthly suffering if heaven isn't our longed-for home. If we are living with comfort in this earthly life as the ultimate goal, and we make little progression in our eternal life with Christ, then most of our deepest sufferings will indeed seem pointless. Suffering is redemptive when we experience it in light of eternity and in the context of God reconciling all the brokenness in creation to Himself; and that is something that I didn't have the theology to fully grasp before I became a Catholic.

It was in the midst of my mother's illness that we faced the prognosis of losing our third child. I shared the story of our son Sam's miraculous healing in chapter 5. It was an unbelievably faith-building phenomenon to walk through, and the experience changed my life forever—but not for the reason you might think. Yes, we got the miracle we were praying for, the one we wanted, the one many people in that situation do not get. The end of the story was *happy*; he didn't die. But, as I tell people often, that wasn't the most significant miracle God accomplished. The greater miracle was the one that was divinely orchestrated within my heart as I faced the approaching suffering and loss. The Father gave my heart peace with His will, *whatever type of pain and suffering that might entail*. I had a personal moment of reckoning with the truth of the Gospel and God's plan to redeem all of humanity. *Was I going to live as though this was all real, as if I truly believed it?* I could either place all of my hope and purpose in God's promise of heaven, or I would struggle through the tragedy and pain of this loss, and probably many others in life, constantly looking over my shoulder at what next calamity might steal my joy or disrupt my peace. The measured, prepared, well-performing woman in me had found herself unavoidably faced with the realization that I was not exempt from suffering, and that no amount of my own power could protect me from it. But I also found myself nose to nose with God's *intimate* faithfulness and the offer of His eternal peace. Would I surrender my suffering up to His will and His *good* plan for my life? It is certainly no less than a miracle to me that my heart made the right choice; I can only attribute the outcome to grace—many sacramental avenues of grace in my life. At one point I remember looking at my husband and saying in earnest, "I'm so grateful to be a Catholic in the midst of this." It was a turning point in my life; I had been confronted with my greatest suffering and worst fears, and the peace of Christ had rooted my soul in the reality of heaven. The Catholic Church had given me an impenetrable shelter, an eternal home of rest for my soul amid the suffering of this life.

But, as we know all too well, suffering is not a *singular* experience in the human life; we can expect to face it again and again. Our peace and hope will be challenged. The enemy will continually seek to take back the ground he has lost, and so we have to again and again surrender our sufferings to Christ. I see quite clearly now that my "yes" to God's will in Sam's story was a preparation and practice for future, harder moments of surrender to come in my life.

It was the fall of 2017, and Mom's condition had declined considerably. She had started having moments of great panic and anxiety; she would regularly forget who my dad was and try to get away from him or me. She even once jumped out of the car while it was stopped at the light in the middle of the highway, due to an overwhelming instinct that she was in danger. There were a lot of other physical challenges that emerged as well. Amidst us facing these realities of the disease's progression, my sister had just discovered Dr. Dale Bredesen's brand new book, *The End of Alzheimer's*, and his astounding research. He had identified what seemed to be the main contributing factors of Alzheimer's, and he had successfully addressed these factors and thus *reversed* the disease in a number of patients. My siblings and I read the book, and we agreed that Dr. Bredesen's "Recode protocol"[103] was certainly worth trying. Dad was on board, which he would have to be to ensure that Mom followed the protocol exactly; and my sister helped with most of the legwork of connecting my parents with a Recode-certified physician who got her started on the protocol. The genetic testing that was involved revealed Mom was in fact positive for *two copies* of the APOE4 allele (the "Alzheimer's gene"), which puts an individual at a statistically probable (50-90 percent) chance of developing Alzheimer's and developing it relatively early (in one's sixties or even earlier). We were optimistic about seeing possible improvement, however, because we had read about many people in Mom's situation (with two copies of the gene as well) who had successfully prevented and reversed Alzheimer's. And in fact, her repeat blood tests after being on the protocol for six months revealed unquestionable improvements in the various contributing factors to the disease. Her anxiety level noticeably improved, and she has lately been making relational connections that she wasn't making before. Time will reveal how much Mom's condition will ultimately improve. But after the suffering she had experienced from this disease, we were hopeful about a protocol that appeared to be improving her quality of life and giving her a fighting chance.

I wish that was the extent of the cross of Alzheimer's in my life, but it is not. In light of Mom's genetic test results, her doctor strongly recommended my siblings and I get tested as well; we would most certainly inherit one copy of the gene from Mom, putting us at a bit of an increased risk of getting the disease ourselves. The week of my birthday in spring of 2018, after having just given birth to our daughter, Stella Maris, three months earlier, I opened the email with my test results. I didn't have one copy of the gene...

I had *two*.

As I looked at the technically worded medical results, it was as if I were reading a parallel email simultaneously that stated: *In thirty years, you will have Alzheimer's like your mom. You will forget your children and your husband. You will lose all of your mental abilities and bodily functions, and it will ultimately take your life.* Fear and dread assailed my senses; but I had a choice, one God had been preparing me for since my suffering with Sam. It was a moment similar to my moment facing the bathroom mirror in the fetal imaging office three years earlier. At that moment, the hope of heaven and the goodness of God's redeeming story were bigger than my looming suffering. Grace rushed in, and I was able to again say "yes" to whatever God's providence held for me: "yes" to the possibility or probability of developing Alzheimer's; "yes" to the inconveniences and small sufferings of a preventative lifestyle; "yes" to an ongoing battle against fear; "yes" to uniting my sufferings with those of Christ's; and "yes" to living my life out of the abundance of God's peace and mercy and not out of my own self-sufficiency. It's a "yes" required of us all, but we put it off. The unseen grace in suffering is that we can put off the "yes" no longer. When we view our lives in this world in the light of eternity we see that whatever plan God has for bringing us and those we love to heaven is a *good* one. And we will view suffering in a redemptive way. But we cannot come to live in this reality if we don't understand and embrace Christ's work on the cross and our own role as members of His body united in His suffering.

Uniting Our Suffering with Christ's

The cross—the universal symbol of both suffering and redemption—bears great significance for our embodied faith. When we Catholics enter a church and gaze ahead at the crucifix we see the image of the One who took on all suffering to redeem humanity. As a Protestant, I had a pretty good understanding of Christ's suffering as the victim for sin in our stead, but not until I became Catholic and understood what was going on in the Mass did I have a theological grasp of the role of *my suffering*. In the Mass and in the Eucharist, we celebrate and participate in the sacrifice of Christ the Son offered up to the Father through the Spirit. Every Mass aligns us with the story of redemption, the cosmic liturgy. Christ came, in our nature, taking on our sin. He was the final and perfect Lamb, the sinless sacrifice to satisfy God's justice. He came to redeem all of God's children—to redeem them from sin and death—into new life *in Him*. Christ is the head, and we all make up His body—the Church. Scripture is constantly reminding us that we are one with Christ, as members of His body.[104] Therefore, the entirety of our lives is to be united to His, and that includes our *suffering* too. In the sacrifice of the Mass we are given the opportunity to actively and continually unite ourselves with Christ's sacrifice to the glory of the Father. The Church expounds on the significance of our participation in Christ's sacrifice:

> The cross is the unique sacrifice of Christ, the "one mediator between God and men." But because in his incarnate divine person he has in some way united himself to every man, "the possibility of being made partners, in a way known to God, in the paschal mystery" is offered to all men. He calls his disciples to "take up [their] cross and follow [him]," for "Christ also suffered for [us], leaving [us] an example so that [we] should follow in his steps." In fact Jesus desires to associate with his redeeming sacrifice those who were to be its first beneficiaries. This is achieved supremely in the case of his mother, who was associated more intimately than any other person in the mystery of his redemptive suffering.[105]

The reason the Mass is central to our Catholic faith is that it is the most perfect and complete prayer, out of which we are to live our lives at all moments. *The Mass embodies our life of faith.* For it makes present the reality that God the Father is to "be glorified in all things through Jesus Christ."[106] Again and again, through the Church's liturgy, sacraments, prayers, and traditions we have seen that the ultimate goal of our lives is unity with the Father, in Christ, through the Spirit—this is the telos of our pilgrim journey with the Church. And Christ wants to redeem and unify every part of our lives to the Father. Yes, even (perhaps *especially*) our sufferings have a role in God's cosmic plan of redeeming all creation to Himself. St. Paul indicates our sufferings of this life, as part of Christ's body, are intended to complete Christ's suffering and by divine design benefit the entire Church body: "I am now rejoicing in my sufferings for your sake, and in my flesh I am completing what is lacking in Christ's afflictions for the sake of his body, that is, the church."[107]

Our suffering and pain in this life, when united with Christ's, has eternal blessedness. It is not wasted; it is not unseen. Author Tyler Blanski puts it this way: "In suffering, Jesus showed us how to suffer. Even more, if we let him, he will suffer in us and we in him... For the baptized faithful pain is not pointless. Sharing in the Paschal Mystery, suffering can be salvific, a compassion."[108] This view of suffering is perhaps the most difficult to live out in our modern world. Our society is one of death denial, existing in a culture of constant distraction from the end that is coming to all of our mortal lives. We are all going to die. *Memento Mori*—"remember you will die"—is the reflection our Church calls us to keep present in our minds and hearts. *We are all going to die.* Some of us will die sooner than later. Some will die in war; some will die in peace. Some will die young from disease; some will die old from organs that have lost their function. My son Sam, and all others who have ever experienced miraculous healing in this life, will *still* die one day. In the scope of eternity, our lives in this world are a mere blink of the eye, and our Church is God's instrument to help us live in the reality of the world to come. Suffering in this life, *redemptive* suffering, is actually a mercy that helps us loosen our grip of this life and live every moment of it with the hope of our eternal home.

Carrying Our Crosses and "Offering It Up"

In light of the cross and Christ's redemption of suffering through it, we have been called to "carry our crosses" and offer ourselves as "living sacrifices" to God *daily*.[109] While I have had moments of grace to be able to offer up heavy crosses, I truly struggle in allowing the little sufferings of daily life to bear eternal fruit. It is the little denials of self that are so hard for most of us, but it is actually in offering those small and consistent sacrifices that we practice holiness and become saints in the kingdom of heaven. Therefore, we start in our daily moments of life to give everything as a sacrifice, and one of the best tools to help us practice this is in praying a Morning Offering. There are many different versions of the Morning Offering, but the emphasis of them all is on uniting all aspects of our day with Jesus' sacrifice in the Mass. Here's such a portion from one traditional version: "…I offer thee all my prayers, works, joys, and sufferings of this day, in union with the Holy Sacrifice of the Mass, offered throughout the world, in reparations for my sins…"[110] I also like the version that Fr. Collins offers: "Jesus, I offer you my day and all that is in it—all the prayers, works, joys, and sufferings I might experience today—in union with your own Heart that is loved by the Father and opened up to the world, even if it gets pierced…"[111]

We should be careful to avoid a kitschy use of the phrase "offer it up," which occurs sometimes in Catholic subculture. I'm not saying we can't have it printed on our coffee mugs, but it is important we approach such an act with reverence. Offering up our little sufferings as a prayerful sacrifice to the Father should not be viewed or done flippantly; our little deaths to self are truly salvific, and we should earnestly offer up every sacrifice—no matter how small—for the purpose of uniting our will completely with God's and bringing Him the ultimate glory. I believe the lives of the saints provide the most practical examples and spiritual inspirations for how we can make these daily offerings. In becoming absorbed in the saints' stories, we can begin to imitate them as they imitate Christ.[112] St. Therese's personal Morning Prayer is a beautiful daily offering to pray:

> O my God! I offer Thee all my actions of this
> day for the intentions and for the glory of the

Sacred Heart of Jesus. I desire to sanctify every beat of my heart, my every thought, my simplest works, by uniting them to Its infinite merits; and I wish to make reparation for my sins by casting them into the furnace of Its Merciful Love. O my God! I ask of Thee for myself and for those whom I hold dear, the grace to fulfill perfectly Thy Holy Will, to accept for love of Thee the joys and sorrows of this passing life, so that we may one day be united together in heaven for all Eternity. Amen.[113]

Though the Church gives us a powerful theological basis for redemptive suffering in our lives, suffering remains a *mystery* to us. And, as Flannery O'Connor has observed with prophetic precision, "Mystery is a great embarrassment to the modern mind."[114] For us to suffer redemptively, unite ourselves with Christ, and live with our hope in heaven, we have to detach ourselves from the facades and false securities to which modernity would anchor us. We must embrace the mystery of salvation and live humbly within the divine tensions and human blind spots that require faith and trust in the goodness of God and in His ultimate redemption of all the world.

Resources for Embodied Faith

The Secret Diary of Elisabeth Leseur: The Woman Whose Goodness Changed Her Husband from Atheist to Priest, by Elisabeth Leseur

Elisabeth Leseur's cause for beatification was started in 1934, and her current status in that process is "Servant of God." Her husband found her diaries after her death, and what she recorded of her spiritual life with God in those pages ultimately led him to become a Catholic priest. Elisabeth endured a great deal of physical suffering throughout her life, and her life was ultimately cut short by illness. Her personal reflections are a powerful witness to redemptive suffering. The daily sacrifices that Elisabeth made were often seen by God alone, but her story reveals immense eternal spiritual fruit in her life and the lives of those closest to her.

Story of a Soul: The Autobiography of St. Therese of Lisieux (translated by John Clarke)

St. Therese has so much to teach us; after all, she is a doctor of the Church. She too is a woman who lived through significant physical (and spiritual) sufferings, and her life reveals a beautiful model for how to offer up those daily sufferings, especially the little ones, in union with Christ's sacred heart. Despite the fact that this woman lived over a century ago within the walls of a convent, her story offers much practical application for the daily moments of our lives today.

3 Moments of the Day, by Fr. Christopher S. Collins, S. J.

This short and easy read describes three powerful "moments" every Catholic can practice daily: The Morning Offering, The Examen, and Living the Eucharist. His discussion of the Morning Offering expounds a good bit on what I have shared here about the significance of uniting everything that happens during our day (including our sufferings) with Christ's sacrifice to the Father. The other two moments he describes are also connected to that daily posture of our hearts, and all three will help us to be unified with God's will.

Conclusion

I have come *home* to the Catholic Church. She has given me the gift of an embodied faith; and, in every season of my life, she points me toward Christ and shows me how to live in this world with my hope in heaven. Through her cosmic liturgy, grace-filled sacraments, and formational traditions, I have been given the power and spiritual sustenance required for me to faithfully walk the path God intends, to one day reach my home in heaven with Him.

There may be readers who are currently seeking a home just as I was. For me, the stories of other seekers were some of the most helpful voices on my journey. Perhaps my experience gives voice to the intuitions or private musings of others who feel homeless, wandering on their pilgrimage from one religious shelter to the next.

Truth will reveal itself to the persistent seeker. *Seek and you will find.* I hope my story may open a path previously hidden to you; perhaps one particular part offers you a door you have not yet tried.

There will also be readers whose experiences resonate with my own. They too know what it means to find their home in the Church, and perhaps it's been the one constant amid a life and world of much change. Perhaps it's been a safe haven during life's storms. Maybe some, like the Prodigal Son in the Gospels, have strayed, but the Church has pulled them back into the arms of the waiting Father. I hope my experience of homecoming inspires those individuals to live out of the home of their Catholicism with renewed faith. May my story, together with the stories of so many others, kindle the flame of love in their hearts for the gift of Christ's Church.

But for some reading these words, the Church has not been a home; it has not been a safe haven. My story may sound foreign to those readers because they have experienced Catholicism as the furthest thing from *home*. Perhaps the broken institution, broken leaders, and broken people they have experienced within the Church's walls have been the greatest stumbling block to their lives of faith.

If this has been your story, then I want you to know that Christ weeps with you, because He loves you, and because the pain they have caused you they have caused to His heart as well. What you have known as "Catholicism" has not been Christ's Church; it has not been His mystical body; it has not been His hands and His feet. The true Church—with her liturgy, her sacraments, her faith, *her God*—waits to be discovered as the true home Christ meant it to be for you here on earth. Know too that through His Church all of your brokenness may be redeemed. God will redeem the years "that the swarming locust has eaten" (Joel 2:25). In God's economy no suffering is wasted, nor is any story beyond redemption.

Whatever your story, may you too be *home* in the Church and live an *abundant*, embodied Catholic faith.

About the Author

J essica Ptomey is a Catholic convert, wife, mom, writer, Communications scholar, and homeschooler. She blogs at jessicaptomey.com and CatholicMom.com, writing about various topics relevant to living intentional lives of faith, communication, and education. Jessica holds a B.A. in Communications from Bryan College (Dayton, TN) and an M.A. in Journalism and Ph.D. in Communication Studies from Regent University (Virginia Beach, VA). She teaches as an online adjunct professor of Communication at Liberty University, and her inter-faith dialogue research has been published in the Journal of Communication and Religion (JCR). She is also the co-host with her husband Mike of The Catholic Reading Challenge podcast. Jessica lives with her husband and their four children in the Maryland suburbs of Washington, DC.

Endnotes

1 C. S. Lewis, *Mere Christianity* (New York: Harper Collins, 2001), xv.

2 James K. A. Smith, *Who's Afraid of Postmodernism?* (Grand Rapids: Baker Academic, 2006), 29.

3 Scholars have traced in detail Protestant American Christianity's roots in modernism. See George M. Marsden, *Fundamentalism and American Culture* (New York: Oxford University Press, 2006); Mark A. Noll, *The Scandal of the Evangelical Mind* (Grand Rapids: Wm. B. Eerdmans Co., 1994); and Ross Douthat, *Bad Religion: How We Became a Nation of Heretics* (New York: Free Press, 2012).

4 James K. A. Smith, *Desiring the Kingdom: Worship, Worldview and Culture Formation* (Grand Rapids: Baker Academic, 2009), 51.

5 Smith, 57.

6 Smith, 89-129.

7 Thomas Aquinas, *Summa Theologica* I-II, 34, a4.

8 Peter Kreeft, *Socrates Meets Kant* (San Francisco: Ignatius Press, 2009), 183.

9 Scott Hahn, *The Lamb's Supper: The Mass as Heaven on Earth* (New York: Doubleday, 1999), 160.

10 Smith, *Desiring the Kingdom,* 51.

11 Two books that were primary influencers were: Christian Smith, *How to Go from Being a Good Evangelical to a Committed Catholic in Ninety-Five Difficult Steps* (Eugene: Cascade Books, 2011) and Scott and Kimberly Hahn, *Rome Sweet Home* (San Francisco: Ignatius Press, 1993).

12 *Catechism of the Catholic Church*, 2nd. ed. (Washington, DC: United States Catholic Conference, 2000), [1136].

13 *Catechism*, [1138].

14 *Catechism*, [1157].

15 *Catechism*, [1358-1361].

16 All Scripture passages are taken from the Revised Standard Version Catholic Edition (RSV-CE), copyrighted 1946, 1952, 1957, 1965, 1966, 2006 by the Division of Christian Education of the National Council of the Churches of Christ in the USA.

17 Bishop Robert Barron, "What is Happening at Mass?" *Word on Fire*, October 10, 2017, https://www.wordonfire.org/resources/article/what-is-happening-at-mass/5609/.

18 *Catechism*, [1146].

19 *Catechism*, [1408].

20 The seven sacraments of the Church are Baptism, Confirmation, Eucharist, Penance, Anointing of the Sick, Holy Orders, and Matrimony. *Catechism of the Catholic Church*, [1113].

21 *Catechism*, [1131].

22 *Catechism*, [1324].

23 *Catechism*, [1140].

24 *Catechism*, [1368].

25 *Catechism*, [1332].

26 *Catechism*, [1419].

27 Hahn, *The Lamb's Supper*, 64.

28 Bishop Robert Barron, *Heaven in Stone and Glass* (New York: Crossroad, 2000), 18-19.

29 Barron, *Heaven in Stone and Glass*, 13.

30 *Catechism*, [776].

31 *Catechism*, [1131].

32 *Catechism*, [1996].

33 *Catechism*, [774].

34 *Catechism*, [775].

35 *Catechism*, [1236].

36 *Catechism*, [1253].

37 *Catechism*, [1254].

38 *Catechism*, [1239.

39 *Catechism*, [1285].

40 *Catechism*, [1303, 1316].

41 *Catechism*, [1295].

42 *Catechism*, [1303].

43 *Catechism*, [1389].

44 1 Corinthians 11:27-29

45 *Catechism*, [980].

46 *Catechism*, [985].

47 *Catechism*, [982].

48 Mother Mary Loyola, *The King of the Golden City*, Special
    Edition for Boys (Homer Glen, IL: St. Augustine Academy Press,
    2017), 23-24.

49 Loyola, *The King of the Golden City*, 38.

50 Matthew 10:1-15

51 *Catechism*, [1513, 1514].

52 *Catechism*, [1555].

53 *Catechism*, [1548].

54 *Catechism*, [1578].

55 *Catechism*, [1566].

56 *Catechism*, [1641-1642].

57 Peter Kreeft, *Jesus Shock* (South Bend, IN: St. Augustine's Press,
    2008), 117.

58 2 Peter 1:3

59 *Catechism*, [1656-1657].

60 *Catechism*, [1666].

61 *Catechism*, [2205].

62 *Catechism*, [2205].

63 *Catechism*, [2685].

64 *Catechism*, [2685].

65 *Catechism*, [2207].

66 *Catechism*, [1168].

67 *Catechism*, [1163], emphasis mine.

68 Romans 6:4

69 "Episode 8: A Vast Company of Witnesses: A Communion of Saints." *Catholicism*, DVD, directed by Matt Leonard (Des Plaines, IL: Word on Fire, 2011).

70 *Catechism*, [1090].

71 Revelation 8:3

72 Revelation 12:17

73 *Catechism*, [2683].

74 *Catechism*, [2617].

75 "The Apostles' Creed," *Catechism of the Catholic Church*, 49-50.

76 *Catechism*, [2558].

77 *Catechism*, [2702].

78 Jim Forester, *Love Is the Measure* (Mahwah, NJ: Paulist Press, 1986), 61.

79 *Catechism*, [2558].

80 John 14:23

81 *Catechism*, [2562].

82 *Catechism*, [2721].

83 *Catechism*, [2722].

84 *Catechism*, [2705-2708].

85 Jeremiah 17:9

86 C. S. Lewis, *Letters to Malcolm: Chiefly on Prayer* (New York: Harcourt, Brace & World, 1964), 20-23.

87 Ezekiel 36:26

88 St. Charles Borromeo, "Acta Ecelesiae Mediolanensis," *Mediolani* 1599, 1177-1178.

89 Matthew 15:19

90 *Catechism*, [2708].

91 *Catechism*, [2724].

92 *Catechism*, [2715].

93 *Catechism*, [2711].

94 *Catechism*, [2643].

95 *Catechism*, [2558].

96 Ephesians 6:18; Luke 21:36

97 *Catechism*, [2697].

98 Psalm 119:164

99 Second Vatican Council, Constitution on the Sacred Liturgy *Sacrosanctum Concilium*, (December 4, 1963) IV, 90, http://www.vatican.va/archive/hist_councils/ii_vatican_council/documents/vat-ii_const_19631204_sacrosanctum-concilium_en.html.

100 *Catechism*, [2710].

101 Luke 6:45

102 John Paul II, *Salvifici Doloris,* apostolic letter (February 11, 1984), no. 19, emphasis in original, https://w2.vatican.va/content/john-paul-ii/en/apost_letters/1984/documents/hf_jp-ii_apl_11021984_salvifici-doloris.html.

103 Dale Bredesen, *The End of Alzheimer's* (New York: Avery, 2017).

104 Romans 12:5; Galatians 3:28; Colossians 3:15

105 *Catechism*, [618].

106 1 Peter 4:11

107 Colossians 1:24

108 Tyler Blanski, *An Immovable Feast* (San Francisco: Ignatius Press, 2018), 147.

109 Luke 9:23; Romans 12:1

110 The Morning Offering. https://www.ewtn.com/devotionals/prayers/morning2.htm

111 Christopher S. Collins, *3 Moments of the Day* (Notre Dame, IN: Ave Maria Press, 2014), 137.

112 1 Corinthians 11:1

113 "A Morning Prayer Written by St. Therese." https://www.ewtn.com/devotionals/prayers/therese3.htm.

114 Flannery O'Connor, *Mystery and Manners* (New York: Farrar, Straus and Giroux, 1969), 124.

CPSIA information can be obtained
at www.ICGtesting.com
Printed in the USA
BVHW031107191119
564088BV00001BA/1/P

9 781642 797084